THE JESSIE AND JOHN DANZ LECTURES

Social Environment and Health

Stewart Wolf

University of Washington Press
Seattle and London

Library of Congress Cataloging in Publication Data

Wolf, Stewart George, 1914–
  Social environment and health.

  (The Jessie and John Danz lectures)
  Based on lectures delivered Feb. 1979 at the
University of Washington, Seattle.
  Bibliography: p.
  1. Social medicine. I. Title. II. Series:
Jessie and John Danz lectures.
RA418.W634   613   80-50868
ISBN 0-295-95777-8

THE JESSIE AND JOHN DANZ LECTURES

In October 1961, Mr. John Danz, a Seattle pioneer, and his wife, Jessie Danz, made a substantial gift to the University of Washington to establish a perpetual fund to provide income to be used to bring to the University of Washington each year "distinguished scholars of national and international reputation who have concerned themselves with the impact of science and philosophy on man's perception of a rational universe." The fund established by Mr. and Mrs. Danz is now known as the Jessie and John Danz Fund, and the scholars brought to the University under its provisions are known as Jessie and John Danz Lecturers or Professors.

Mr. Danz wisely left to the Board of Regents of the University of Washington the identification of the special fields in science, philosophy, and other disciplines in which lectureships may be established. His major concern and interest were that the fund would enable the University of Washington to bring to the campus some of the truly great scholars and thinkers of the world.

Mr. Danz authorized the Regents to expend a portion of the income from the fund to purchase special collections of books, documents, and other scholarly materials needed to reinforce the effectiveness of the extraordinary lectureships and professorships. The terms of the gift also provided for the publication and dissemination, when this seems appropriate, of the lectures given by the Jessie and John Danz Lecturers.

Through this book, therefore, another Jessie and John Danz Lecturer speaks to the people and scholars of the world, as he has spoken to his audiences at the University of Washington and in the Pacific Northwest community.

Preface

This book is based on the Jessie and John Danz Lectures delivered during February 1979 at the University of Washington, Seattle. I acknowledge with gratitude the warm hospitality of Dr. Ronald Geballe, Dean of the Graduate School, and of Mrs. Marjorie Geballe. Among my sponsors and hosts, I express special thanks to Dr. and Mrs. John A. Schilling, Dr. and Mrs. Robert G. Petersdorf, Dr. Herbert S. Ripley, Dr. and Mrs. Thomas H. Holmes, Dr. and Mrs. Leonard P. Eliel, and the Chiefs of Service and Residents at the University of Washington affiliated hospitals with whom I worked with such profit and pleasure.

In the lectures, I attempted to synthesize available data linking the quality of social relationships to physical health and disease, and thereby to clarify one aspect of human ecology. I reviewed contributions from several disciplines among the medical, biological, and social sciences—disciplines that ordinarily do not intercommunicate—and documented my views with a broad range of descriptive epidemiological and experimental studies extending from antiquity to the present. My thesis emphasized the integrative functions of the central nervous system in regulating adaptive responses to environmental challenges of all sorts, concrete and symbolic. A smooth, well-modulated adaptive response was seen as equivalent to health, while exaggerated, insufficient, or inappropriate responses in the various organ systems were identified as the very manifestations of disease. Throughout this analysis, I stressed the importance of intercommunication and interdependence in the process of social and biological homeostasis.

I hope this book will be enlightening to those about to undertake the study of medicine as well as students in other biological sciences and in the social sciences. Perhaps, too, there may be something of interest for the student of philosophy and for the student of life, the intelligent and inquisitive layman.

I acknowledge with great pleasure the contribution of Helen Goodell throughout the development of this book. Her penetrating insights, her wise critiques, and her encouragement have been invaluable. I am also grateful to the administration and Board of Trustees of St. Luke's Hospital of Bethlehem, Pennsylvania, who afforded me the time and resources to prepare the lectures and this book. Special thanks go to Mrs. Joy Colarusso Lowe for her skill and unflagging patience in preparing the manuscript and to Mr. John Levko, who reproduced many of the illustrations.

Contents

Social Environment and Health

1. The Concept of Adaptation and Health

I hope to support the proposition that effective social adjustment that yields personal satisfaction and fulfillment is conducive to health and that social failure, frustration, dissatisfaction, deprivation, and disapproval enhance vulnerability to disease. The idea is not new. Neither is it widely accepted.

Although it is easily acknowledged that man, as a tribal creature, depends on his fellows for recognition, support, and understanding, the hypothesis that the quality of his social adjustment is pertinent to his health and longevity has not been incorporated into the mainstream of biomedical scientific thought. Nor is it likely to be unless and until there develops some solid understanding as to how social forces can actually affect the function and structure of bodily organs. That understanding, still not fully at hand, has nevertheless been building rapidly in recent years. Studies of animals and man have yielded three classes of evidence: descriptive, often called anecdotal; epidemiologic; and experimental. The interpretation of such evidence depends, of course, on prevailing attitudes and assumptions about health and disease and about man's relationship to his world (Fabrega 1979).

3

CONCEPTS OF DISEASE

Over the course of recorded history, man's view of disease has vacillated, focusing alternately on the contributions of outside agents (evil spirits, bad air, microbes) and on defects in the sick individual himself. The former theory has been called xenochthonous from the Greek Xenos, stranger or outsider, and the latter autochthonous, reflecting the focus on self.

Another belief, also ancient and perhaps more persuasive, holds that disease results, not from outside forces alone or simply from deficiencies in the affected individual, but rather is the consequence of interaction between the two. The latter view was essentially that propounded by the ancient Chinese. For them health reflected a proper balance between opposing forces called Yin and Yang, while disease was caused by a lack

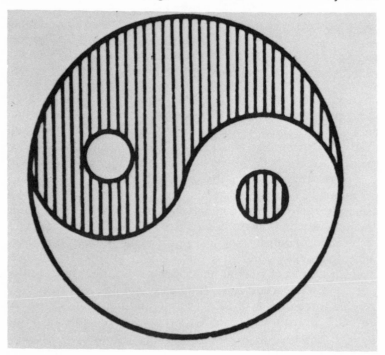

Figure 1. The traditional representation of Yin and Yang

of balance between the two. The Greeks in the pre-Christian era also saw health as a balance of reciprocal forces. More recent concepts, stemming from the revolutionary discoveries of microbiologists in the nineteenth century, Pasteur, Koch, and others, led us back to the xenochthonous view that disease is something inflicted on man by outside forces. The fact that a microbe may strike down an apparently healthy person strengthened the conviction that disease must come from the outside. More recently, the view that the proclivity for disease is essentially inherent in the individual himself has gained support from our rapidly burgeoning understanding of genetics. Lately, however, a position somewhat akin to that of the ancient Chinese and the Greeks has been proposed under the banner of ecology. The ecological view holds that disease is a consequence of interaction between the person and his environment and that health, therefore, is manifested by a behavior of bodily systems that achieves and maintains a comfortable relationship with the environment. I hope to defend here a further proposition that the manifestations of disease are themselves evidences of biological adaptations to potential agents of disease, environmental challenges, including challenges in the psychosocial sphere.

BEHAVIOR

Behavior, in its broadest sense, is the very expression of adaptation. Thus, for our purposes, behavior is viewed as the expressive use of the machinery of the body in a purposeful and goal-directed way to fulfill desires and aspirations, to express inborn drives for comfort and survival, or to respond to an external cue or stimulus. Those activities performed by skeletal muscles—walking, running, gesturing, facial expressions, fighting, writing, and speaking—are governed by impulses from somatic nerves and constitute only a part of behavior. Weeping and blushing are also obvious features of behavior. The lacrimal glands that provide tears and the blood vessels of the face responsible for blushing are activated by autonomic nerves, sympathetic and parasympathetic, the same system of nerves that governs the heartbeat, the secretions of the endocrine glands, the movements and secretions of the digestive tract, and the excretory functions of the kidneys and bladder. The autonomic nerves provide the less obvious, more recondite aspects of behavior, but are nevertheless as much involved in adaptive responses of all sorts as are the somatic nerves that control the skeletal muscles.

Recognizing the importance of adaptation to health, J. B. S. Haldane declared: "Progress in medicine depends on understanding how the human organism adapts to changes in his environment" (Haldane and Priestley 1935). As mentioned above, I would further suggest that the adaptations of the human organism, when exaggerated, insufficient, or inappropriate in some way, actually *constitute* the manifestations of disease. For example, a healthy person living at altitude, as in the Andes, maintains a substantially elevated red blood cell count, thereby compensating for the diminished atmospheric pressure of oxygen. The additional red cells are needed to deliver adequate oxygen to the tissues. When such a rise in red cell count occurs at sea level, however, the increase is inappropriate and a disease, polycythemia, is present. The bodily mechanisms required to increase the number of circulating red blood cells are nevertheless identical in both situations, in health and disease. As another example, a heart rate of 120 in a runner immediately after a 100-yard dash would be considered a sign of health, but in a bedridden or even sedentary patient the same heart rate would be a clear evidence of illness. Similarly, Graves' disease, or hyperthyroidism, consists of the excessive elaboration of a normal, indeed an essential, hormone. As a further example, diabetes involves the substitution of a ketone for a glucose metabolism, which in the face of starvation is a normal and effective metabolic adaptation. When a person is well fed, however, such a metabolic behavior signals the potentially fatal hazard of uncompensated diabetes.

THE ROOTS OF BIOLOGICAL ADAPTATION

The bodily equipment that has enabled man to cope successfully with the multitude of forces around him has evolved through genetic mutation over the long course of biologic evolution. The most highly successful structures and mechanisms, the pick of countless mutations, have been preserved and incorporated to serve various purposes in plants and animals all along the phylogenetic scale. Among the most useful and versatile of such biological developments are the tiny hair-like structures called cilia that line your respiratory passages and mine. Beating at a rate of 16 strokes per second, they sweep inhaled dust and other foreign material back up to the nose and mouth. Cilia are among the phylogenetically oldest specialized cellular structures that adapt living organisms to their environment. Acting as oars, they provide locomotion for many protozoa, the paramecia for example, which most of us encountered in our high school biology course. In contrast, the cilia of oysters and other mollusks sweep food contained in seawater into the digestive tract. Despite the widely varied role of this engineering marvel, the basic design of cilia has persisted without modification for many hundreds of millions of years.

As multicellular organisms have increased in size and their complexity has multiplied, evolutionary developments have made possible a host of protective metabolic and circulatory adjustments as well as extraordinarily complex and efficient immune mechanisms that protect against environmental hazards, including microbial invaders and, perhaps, potential carcinogens. Thus an insufficiency in the body's immune apparatus may increase susceptibility to invaders and hence enhance the likelihood of certain infections and possibly cancer (Twomey and Good 1978). Indeed, the difference between infection and mere exposure to microbes depends on a neat balance of activation and restraint of immunological and other defense mechanisms. For some the balance is altogether salubrious, since even in the most devastating epidemic there is always a segment of the exposed population that remains

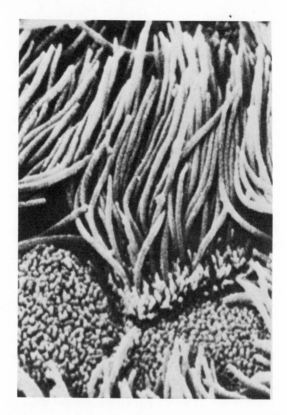

Figure 2. Cilia arising from cells of the human respiratory tree (courtesy of the American Lung Association)

healthy. Their immune mechanisms appear to be finely tuned, neither inadequate nor excessive. Excessive immune responses may result in certain connective tissue diseases, among them lupus erythematosus and rheumatoid arthritis (Samter 1978).

Evolutionary Developments other than Genetic

The enormous adaptive capacity of human beings has been achieved, not only through genetic mutation, but also, thanks

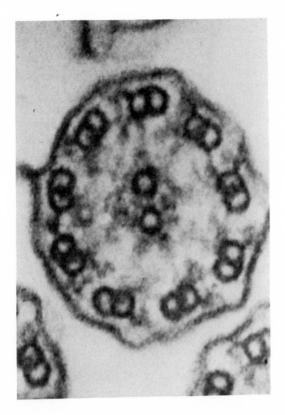

Figure 3. An electron micrograph showing the basic structure of a cilium in cross section (courtesy of Dr. Richard Coggeshall)

to the development of language, through the verbal transmission of the experience of earlier generations, including learning, customs, and values. The method of transmission was first oral, and later in writing as well. Human behaviors, attitudes, and responses are also shaped by nonverbal communications, especially during experiences in infancy and early life, and by the discriminative powers of intelligence, thanks to the capacity of the human brain for learning and for making and testing judgments and decisions. Along with the evolution of the intellect there has occurred a rich proliferation in the emotional sphere manifested in artistic creativity and responsiveness to a broad range of aesthetic experiences as well as more earthy emotions concerned with personal fulfillment, competitiveness, ambition, greed, envy, fear, etc. These and other human qualities participate in the process by which a person adapts to his surroundings. Too much or too little of any adaptive function, insofar as the individual's physiological behavior is inappropriate, may contribute toward disease. Therefore, whether health or illness prevails appears to be determined by the algebraic sum of numerous relevant behavior determinants acting over time. Important among them are genetic endowment, early life experience, and encounters over the years with myriad potentially harmful agents and forces, tangible and intangible, that characterize one's environment.

SOCIAL ADAPTATION

For modern man in Western civilization, adaptation to his social environment appears to offer greater challenge than does his adaptation to the physical environment which, except for devastating natural disasters and the hazards of industrial and other environmental poisons, has become largely neutralized by such stratagems as central heating, air conditioning, and public hygiene. The concept of successful social adaptation presupposes that a person has a sense of personal worth and a secure feeling of belonging, of having a role in the scheme of things.

A report from the Harvard University Health Services established with fair certainty that the familiar physical depredations of aging are delayed among those who in their younger years were self-possessed, optimistic, and confident, and occur sooner among those who in adolescence were troubled, uncertain, and chronically anxious. The study comprised more than 200 men who were freshmen at Harvard forty years ago and at the time were considered by the Health Services to be free of any mental or physical disorder. It had been possible to follow 188 of them with annual or biennial questionnaires and periodic interviews. Eighty-three percent of the group after the age of fifty underwent a thorough physical examination by the investigators. Several early tests of psychological adjustment had predicted the state of health of the men when they reached their fifties. Among those who thirty-five years after the initial tests were chronically ill or dead, poor scores were encountered twice as frequently as among those in excellent health (Vaillant 1979). The differences were significant even after eliminating the possible effects of obesity, alcohol and tobacco use, and parents' and grandparents' health.

The implications of a good social adjustment for health and longevity were recognized in a *Report of a Special Task Force to the Secretary of HEW,* published in 1973. It stated, "the strongest predictor of longevity was work satisfaction. The second best predictor over-all 'happiness.'" These two judgmental nonquantitative sociopsychological measures predicted longevity better than a rating by an examining physician of physical functioning, or a measure of tobacco use or genetic inheritance. This report and the Harvard Health Services study, among others, reflect the salubrious consequences of a lifelong pattern of equanimity and effective coping with prevailing circumstances. Richard Lazarus has provided strong evidence for the relationship of one's style of coping to the state of his health (Lazarus 1976). One's capacity for successful coping may be greatly enhanced through human understanding, love, and companionship (Lynch 1977). One prototype of the healthy, long-lived, fulfilled person may be the fine symphony conductor, an individual who is persistently responsive to physical, intellectual, and aesthetic challenges and, also, who is more or less continuously the recipient of approbation from his audiences.

2. Social Forces: Stresses and Supports

The impact of social forces can best be seen during attempts of a community to adapt to rapid social change. In 1938 in a book entitled *Civilization and Disease*, C. P. Donnison, who had worked for many years as a physician in black Africa, reported that he had encountered no hypertension, diabetes, or peptic ulcer in remote areas of the continent where the prevailing social structure was relatively stable. However, these and other chronic diseases did appear where "civilizing" forces were rapidly invading an established culture.

W. L. Brown in his introduction to Donnison's perceptive monograph states in his first sentence, "Physically, the evolution of Man appears to be at a standstill, and it would be a bold man who would maintain that mentally there has been an advance since the days of the ancient Greeks. It is on the psychological side, by which man adjusts himself to his environment, that we can alone expect progress to be made" (p. v).

Donnison's book develops the idea that as man has lived in groups of increasing size, social patterns have evolved to deal with prevailing circumstances, and, over the course of history and in various parts of the world, social structures have been altered and remodeled to meet changing circumstances. When the speed of change has outrun the pace of adaptation, Donnison holds that man's internal mechanisms, mental and physical, acting inappropriately, have provided what he calls the basis of the diseases of civilization.

Donnison's essentially speculative conclusions have received support from evidence gathered in the last forty years indicating that the neural and hormonal mechanisms that characterize essential hypertension, the metabolic manifestations of diabetes and Graves' disease and the gastric acid secretion of peptic ulcer may be elicited as part of a person's reaction to psychologically threatening events (Hinkle, Conger, and Wolf 1950; Hetzel 1964; Wolf 1949). Such evidence, emerging from the studies of Claude Bernard, I. Pavlov, and W. B. Cannon, was extended in clinical and experimental studies on human beings by Harold Wolff and a long list of his followers. The findings are summarized in his book *Stress and Disease* (1953).

Ten years after Donnison's book appeared and coincident with Wolff's studies, J. L. Halliday in England picked up the idea of the potential pathogenicity of social forces and wrote a book called *Psychosocial Medicine* (1948). Halliday argued that although it was obvious to everyone that attention to the physical environment had made possible some of the most effective public health measures—the control of typhoid fever, cholera, plague, typhus, and other infectious diseases, and more recently the control of radiation and of pathogenic chemicals in the environment—similar concern with the psychological and social environment, however appropriate, had lagged behind.

Both Donnison and Halliday saw morale, or common purpose, as the healthy integrating force in society. They both considered disease the consequence of demoralization related to social change, change too swift or too disruptive for the adaptive capacity of the social group.

L. W. Simmons and Harold Wolff, dealing with this issue in their book *Social Science in Medicine* (1954), observed that in decaying cultures anxiety-producing factors tend to outlast those that protect against or relieve anxiety. Similarly Rene Dubos showed that vulnerability to infectious diseases may be enhanced in a setting of rapid social change (Dubos 1951). After a lifetime of study of tuberculosis, he concluded that unsanitary conditions, crowding, poverty, and so forth were less significant in outbreaks of the disease throughout the world than what he referred to as "social disruption," rapid social change. Many other scientists have added confirmation to the concept that the quality of social adaptation is pertinent to health. Indeed, this basic proposition has cropped up repeatedly since antiquity. Nevertheless, it is still not wholly acceptable to the biomedical community, and has yet to be incorporated in currently prevailing thought about medicine and public health.

The increasing emphasis on the significance of homeostatic mechanisms of all sorts has made it easier to accept the proposition that perturbation of an established system may set in motion a destructive chain of events. Thus, an organism adapted to past circumstances is always to some extent maladapted to new circumstances. Daniel Bruner studied oriental Jews who were immigrating to Israel and found that shortly after arrival they had practically no heart attacks. Moreover, those who died in the early years following immigration showed at autopsy practically no arteriosclerosis in their coronary vessels. Recently, however, Bruner observed that the oriental Jews have begun to have coronary artery disease, myocardial infarction (heart attack), and sudden death in rapidly increasing numbers. He points to the extraordinarily rapid social change that has occurred among them (Bruner 1968).

The oriental Jew, living in a tent in the desert in Africa with his wife and children, was an absolute czar of the family. Suddenly in Israel his children were thrown into school where they associated with peer groups that emphasized, as they do in this country, "doing your own thing" and freedom. Therefore, at home, instead of showing their former automatic deference and respect to their fathers, they behaved the way your children and mine do. Moreover, the wife, who in the desert had been covered up literally and figuratively, could now exploit her skills at sewing and cooking to land a job. On the job, surrounded by the ambience of women's "lib," she might also defy her husband. One does not have to be a psychiatrist to visualize the intensity of emotional stress experienced by these oriental Jewish families.

Thomas Holmes, a professor on the faculty of the University of Washington, has made a landmark contribution to the understanding of the pathogenic effects of change. With his student and collaborator, Richard Rahe, he perfected a quantitative scale whereby one can relate emotionally significant social changes to the statistical risk of developing disease (Holmes and Rahe 1967). Holmes and Rahe found that those whose lives had been disrupted to some extent by major events such as the death of a spouse or the loss of a job, and even by less dramatic changes such as assuming a financial debt or taking a vacation, were at increased risk of illness of all sorts. The various "life changes," as they were called, were rated as to their potental significance. The Holmes and Rahe scale has been applied to several different cultures and nationalities around the globe, and has been found generally reliable as a predictor of susceptibility to illness.

The European common market has provided an interesting laboratory for the study of the pathologic effects of radical social change. E. Uehlinger found that while Italians living in Italy had a very low incidence of myocardial infarction, the rate was higher among Italians working in Germany, an incidence comparable to that of their German comrades (Uehlinger 1970). It may be that they were eating much better, but it does not seem likely that diet could have increased the occurrence of myocardial infarction in so short a time. On the other hand, their social change was radical and rapid and thus, without doubt, difficult to adjust to.

Seguin has made similar observations in South America. While studying the industrial setting in Lima, Peru, he found that the workers displaced from the rural areas in the mountains to Lima not only had more heart disease, but more disease of all kinds than did their neighbors back home (Seguin 1956).

Genetic Influence

In a certain variety of rheumatoid arthritis, in diabetes, and in some other conditions, a genetic connection and even the mode of inheritance have been established (McKusick and Claiborne 1973). Penetrance of most genetic disorders, however, requires the addition of one or more contributory environmental factors. Although identical twins carry identical genes associated with a given disease, only one may fall ill. Thus, the presence of a genetic proclivity does not diminish the importance of environmental forces that may lead to disease. Prominent among such environmental forces are social stresses including deprivation, oppression, abuse, and even aging in a youth-oriented culture such as ours. Moreover, the clinical course of some genetic diseases, hemophilia for example, is closely related to the timing of changes in life situation and emotional state of the patient (Hampton 1965). Conversely, susceptibility to social stresses and to other environmental noxae depends in part on genetic inheritance. Indeed, a familial and presumably genetic tendency has been shown in several diseases usually considered to be related in part to emotional stresses—migraine, hypertension, duodenal ulcer, and asthma, for example (Wolf and Goodell 1968).

Social Organization and Social Supports

As pointed out above, early adversities in addition to genetic characteristics may make some individuals more vulnerable to disease than others. A crucial question asks, "What are the factors that protect those who, whatever the circumstances, remain healthy?" The answer may be found, as Donnison suggests, in the concept of "good morale." Morale is a group phenomenon frequently evident in a family with a new infant. Based on common purpose, it reflects the mutual support and approval of family and other positive associations, and implies a sense of belonging and of contributing to others. Good morale may be nourished by strong shared religious beliefs, or by established customs and predictable systems of reward and punishment—essentially by each person knowing and understanding his place in the social organization.

A few years ago in the jungles of Brunei, Borneo, I observed a situation reminiscent of Donnison's experience in Africa (Wolf and Wolf 1978). During a period of rapid social change, diabetes, coronary disease, and hypertension, formerly rare, had begun to affect the inhabitants of the city. The rural tribes, however, who had held tenaciously to their centuries-old social customs, their communal living patterns in longhouses, and their animistic religion, had remained unaffected by these diseases despite the incursions of modern civilization. Since World War II, Brunei had been undergoing drastic changes brought on by its new riches from the discovery of

Figure 4. Map of Southeast Asia showing tiny Brunei between the Malaysian states of Sabah and Sarawak on the island of Borneo

Figure 5. An Iban longhouse nestled in the jungle in Brunei (photo by Hedda Morrison, courtesy of Borneo Literature Bureau)

offshore oil. Even in the rural areas, major social changes were taking place, stemming from the availability of jobs in the oil and lumber industries, or on the crews building roads that penetrated deeply into the jungle. Modern medicine was brought to every community by helicopter, and public health programs had virtually eliminated most tropical and other infectious diseases. Perhaps the most striking change of all was that schools had sprung up everywhere. It is too early to predict whether or not the healthy tribes of Borneo will ultimately succumb to the metabolic and vascular diseases so familiar to us. They should be studied prospectively as a younger generation emerges, a generation that may discard the sustaining traditional beliefs and the established way of life of their parents.

An opportunity to make such a prospective study was available much closer to home in the form of an experiment of nature in Roseto, an Italian community in eastern Pennsylvania (Bruhn and Wolf 1979). We found that this community, which had clung to its "Old World" culture since immigration in 1882 and until the mid 1960s, had enjoyed relative freedom from heart attacks. In fact, the death rate from heart attack in Roseto was less than half that in neighboring communities. Interestingly, the prevalence of usually-accepted risk factors

Figure 6. Close-up of an Iban longhouse (photo by Tom Wolf)

Figure 7. An important gathering in a longhouse (photo by Hedda Morrison, courtesy of Borneo Literature Bureau)

for heart attacks—i.e., consumption of animal fats, smoking, lack of exercise, hypertension, and diabetes—was at least as great in Roseto as in neighboring towns where more than twice as many heart attacks were occurring and where the death rate from heart attack was similar to that of the United States at large. What distinguished the residents of Roseto were their deep religious convictions, their deference and respect for the elderly, the subordination of the women to their

Figure 8. An oil rig off the north coast of Brunei (photo by Tom Wolf)

men, and the high value placed on community, conformity, and the maintenance of symbols of their Italian heritage, including the egalitarian, classless attitude of villagers (*paesani*). The result was a remarkably cohesive social structure where no one was ever emotionally abandoned and where everyone had a well-defined place in the scheme of things. Figures 12, 13, and 14 show the town and townspeople during the early 1960s.

The apparent resistance to a major disease of Western civilization observed in both Brunei and Roseto appears to be related to the tenacity with which traditional beliefs, including religious convictions, were held. Such attitudes, as they shape the values of a culture, determine in large part the behavior of the social group. Deeply ingrained belief systems establish and delineate taboos and social rewards. This is particularly true of religious beliefs and concepts of the relationship of individuals with their Deity. In the Christian tradition, great importance is assigned to aspiration toward moral perfection and, because one inevitably fails in this, to an acceptance of divine grace or forgiveness for imperfections and transgres-

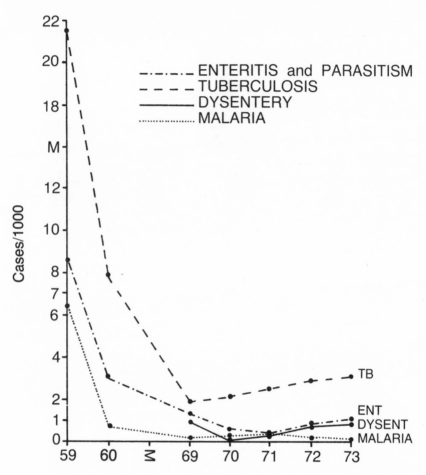

Figure 9. The declining incidence of several diseases from 1959 to 1973 in Brunei

sions for which a person is penitent. In the Christian doctrine of penitence, health equates directly with one's state of grace.

In Roseto there is an annual celebration of penitence on the occasion of the Festival of Our Lady of Mt. Carmel. For years the entire community joined a procession on foot through the

Figure 10. A rural schoolroom in Brunei (photo by Tom Wolf)

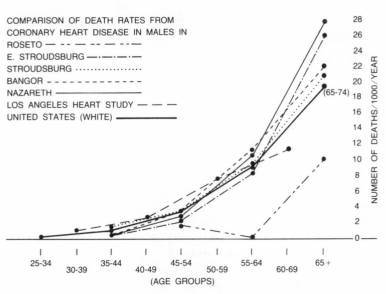

COMPARISON OF DEATH RATES FROM
CORONARY HEART DISEASE IN MALES IN
ROSETO — -- — -- — --—
E. STROUDSBURG —·—·—·—
STROUDSBURG ··················
BANGOR - - - - - - - - - - -
NAZARETH ————————————
LOS ANGELES HEART STUDY — — —
UNITED STATES (WHITE) ——————

NUMBER OF DEATHS/1000/YEAR

28
26
24
22
20
(65-74) 18
16
14
12
10
8
6
4
2
0

25-34 30-39 35-44 40-49 45-54 50-59 55-64 60-69 65+
(AGE GROUPS)

Figure 11. Death rates from myocardial infarction in several age
ranges from 1955 through 1961 in various communities

Figure 12. The procession of the annual Festival of Our Lady of Mt. Carmel, Roseto, Pennsylvania (photo by Remsen Wolff)

whole length of the town. Many marched barefoot to express their humility and gratitude for divine blessings.

In 1963 we noted that most Rosetans under age thirty were paying only lip service to their long-established traditions and social values. We therefore suspected an imminent change in prevailing attitudes and behavior, and in the social structure of the town. In fact, already the number of marchers in the procession during the Festival of Our Lady of Mt. Carmel had decreased, with many young Rosetans watching from the sidewalks. At that time we had the temerity to predict that with the erosion of Old World values, and the abandonment of established social attitudes and customs, the community

Figure 13. A Roseto family at table (photo by Steve Shapiro)

Figure 14. A street in Roseto (photo by Remsen Wolff)

would lose its relative immunity to death from heart attack. Twelve years later, in 1975, we were able to show that our prediction had been correct. With a striking social change characterized by weakening of family ties, a breakaway from ethnic tradition, and adoption of the materialistic values of American society, the death rate from heart attack had climbed to that of the neighboring communities and of the nation at large (Bruhn and Wolf 1979).

Thus it would appear that not only the inherent traits of an individual establish his vulnerability to disease, but equally significant are the prevailing social circumstances and rules of behavior, determined in large part by collective beliefs and religious and ethnic convictions. On the other hand, when social circumstances engender self-confidence and feelings of security, they appear to exert a stabilizing effect on the body's machinery. Perhaps it is from forces akin to these that the subtle but vastly important doctor-patient relationship gains its therapeutic potential.

3. Experimental Studies: Manifestations of Adaptive Behavior

The epidemiologic data resulting from the study of Roseto and of the other communities referred to in the preceding chapter provide, of course, the evidence of coincidence. But despite the correctness of our prediction in Roseto, and since such experiments of nature are uncontrolled and not susceptible to replication, they leave open the possibility of other explanations of the observed events.

In animal experiments, on the other hand, and occasionally in human studies, it has been possible to isolate and control the surrounding circumstances sufficiently to allow for repeated testing and for replication by independent investigators. For example, it has been repeatedly shown that while a large percentage of monkeys harbor the parasite toxoplasma, most remain well. When cage changes are made, however, that alter the social arrangement among the monkeys, toxoplasmosis emerges as a disease (Koprowski 1952).

Herpes simplex virus, like the toxoplasma of monkeys, is harbored for years by healthy people, but may produce fever blisters not only during fevers but accompanying stresses of all sorts, including emotional stress (Blank and Brody 1950; Heilig and Hoff 1928; Schneck 1947).

Among the most interesting and convincing work with animals has been that of J. P. Henry and associates summarized in a volume called *Stress, Health and the Social Environment* (1977). With extraordinary ingenuity these workers arranged a variety of social circumstances for colonies of mice placed in aversive situations for prolonged periods. The animals developed vascular changes, including accelerated arteriosclerosis, hypertension, and glomerular lesions in the kidneys.

C. G. Gunn and collaborators produced accelerated arteriosclerosis in rabbits by electrical stimulation in various regions of the brain, including the hypothalamus, thus providing a possible neural link between psychologically significant stresses and tissue damage (Gunn, Friedman, and Byers 1960). Recent studies reported by R. M. Rose and collaborators have shown that air traffic controllers, constantly facing the hazard of making the wrong decision, are vastly more susceptible to peptic ulcer and high blood pressure than are comparable individuals from other occupations (Rose, Jenkins and Hurst 1978). Others reported a rash of heart attacks among young engineers at Cape Canaveral (Eliot et al. 1976). These men, enthusiastically dedicated to the space program, had suddenly become thoroughly demoralized as they found themselves without a job when the federal government decided to cut back the manned space program. It was particularly difficult for these young people to get another job because their engineering activity had been so highly specialized.

Striking observations such as those described above are often dismissed as anecdotal and accorded little significance, because the intermediary mechanisms responsible for the bodily disorders are not apparent. It seems evident, nevertheless, despite our ignorance of the intermediary mechanisms, that the air traffic controllers who succumbed to hypertension and the space engineers who died suddenly were somehow vulnerable to the "slings and arrows of outrageous fortune."

A vivid example of the importance of surrounding circumstances to the maintenance of health is evident in the observations of B. A. Kakulas and R. D. Adams on a form of muscular dystrophy encountered among quokkas, rodent mar-

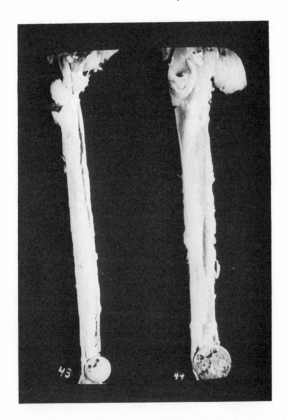

Figure 15. Aortas from rabbits in a study by C. G. Gunn et al. (1960). The aorta on the left showing atherosclerotic plaques is from a rabbit who had had hypothalamic stimulation. The aorta on the right, clear of lesions, is from a control animal.

supials that inhabit western Australia (Kakulas and Adams 1966). Most quokkas live on a small island just off the coast where the vegetation is deficient in vitamin E. The quokkas nevertheless do not develop muscular degeneration in the wild, but only when they are kept in captivity and fed their normal, vitamin E–deficient diet.

Other data are available from the studies of B. Lown, R. Verrier, and R. Corbalan on experimentally induced disturbances in the rhythm of the heartbeat in dogs (Lown, Verrier, and Corbalan 1973). The rhythm disturbances, consisting of runs of premature ventricular beats similar to those encountered in people following a heart attack, were induced in the dogs by electrical stimulation of the heart muscle itself through previously implanted electrodes. The investigators found that the amount of current required to produce the disturbance when delivered to the dog as he rested comfortably in his cage was five times that sufficient to produce the effect when the dog was stimulated in the "alien" environment of the laboratory.

J. E. Skinner and his collaborators obtained comparable findings from experiments on pigs (Skinner, Lie, and Entman 1975). Skinner encircled one of the coronary arteries of each pig with a ligature, bringing the ends of the thread out through the skin so that the artery could be occluded later on while the pig was conscious and after it had fully recovered from the operation. Skinner observed that the occurrence of potentially fatal ventricular fibrillation following ligation of a major coronary artery varied inversely with the degree to which the animals had been made accustomed to the laboratory, the equipment, and the investigators. In fact, ventricular fibrillation occurred promptly following occlusion of the coronary artery in nearly all pigs unfamiliar with the laboratory setting. However, the incidence of ventricular fibrillation was significantly lower among those pigs which, before ligation, had had the experience of four daily visits to the experimental room with no manipulation being undertaken. Those pigs allowed to become accustomed to the laboratory for as long as eight days prior to the experimental procedure were almost fully protected from serious cardiac arrhythmia upon coronary artery ligation (Skinner, Lie, and Entman 1975).

From these and other studies, it has been possible to demonstrate experimentally the salutary effects of familiarity and reassurance on vulnerability to such serious bodily disturbances as cardiac arrhythmias. The conclusion seems evident that vital functions of the body are subject to powerful influence from the parts of the brain that are concerned with thoughts and feelings.

ANTICIPATORY BODILY RESPONSES

Intermediary mechanisms that enable the cerebral cortex, the thinking part of the brain, to control the organs of the body become apparent to the layman in several familiar anticipatory reactions, for example, secretion of saliva in *anticipation* of eating. There are countless other examples of bodily reactions occurring in anticipation: the heartbeat of athletes speeds up prior to running; the secretion of gastric juice is enhanced at the thought of a choice steak.

Several years ago some colleagues and I observed among transfusion donors a particularly illustrative example of less obvious anticipatory visceral behavior (Wolf et al. 1955). In order to compensate for the loss of a half liter of blood, and thereby maintain an adequate level of blood pressure, there occurs in the donor at the time of transfusion an automatic and widespread constriction of small arteries, which maintains blood pressure in the face of blood loss by reducing the space in the body occupied by blood. As shown in figure 16, when

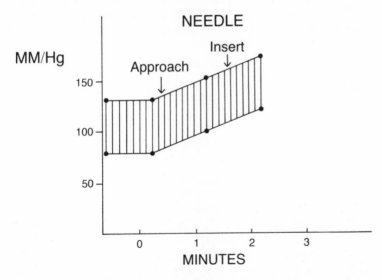

Figure 16. Elevation of systolic and diastolic blood pressure during preparation for withdrawal of blood from a transfusion donor

widespread arterial constriction occurs in the absence of blood loss, blood pressure is actually elevated. We observed such arterial constriction with blood pressure elevation in some transfusion donors before any blood was drawn, in *anticipation* of the blood loss. In fact, in some individuals this occurred merely at the approach of the needle. Thus circulatory adjustments were invoked by a meaningful situation that implied the threat of blood loss.

In other experiments we were able to induce elevated blood pressure and constriction of small arteries of the kidney, and hence a reduction of renal blood flow, during a discussion of intimate personal conflicts with no implication whatever of blood loss. Significantly, while the blood pressure elevation subsided following the stressful discussion and during efforts at reassurance, the reduction of renal blood flow persisted for a time, outlasting the stress (Wolf et al. 1955).

Other workers have documented structural alterations in blood vessels, including arteriosclerosis brought about by sustained vasoconstriction (Schmitt et al. 1970). Although it is not possible as yet to implicate these phenomena in the causal chain of events that leads to essential hypertension and its well-known complications, they do identify a physiological mechanism capable of producing a relatively prolonged disturbance.

Effects of Symbols—"As if" Reactions

The vascular responses described above, triggered by a thought or by a perception of one's surroundings, are attributable to symbolic, as contrasted with tangible, stimuli. The bodily changes observed constitute a part of one's behavior, governed by the personal significance of the situation. Indeed, human beings have a vast repertoire of behaviors that enable them to adapt to life experiences of all sorts. Each involves discrete patterned responses that are activated and coordinated by the nervous system and may involve voluntary as well as involuntary behavior. Against cold, for example, a person may engage in such deliberate activities as putting on a sweater or turning up the heat. If these fail, he will begin to shiver, a reflex behavior that involves skeletal muscle contractions together with constriction of cutaneous blood vessels, an associated autonomically-innervated visceral behavior by which body heat is conserved.

At times, shivering and the constriction of cutaneous blood vessels may occur in *anticipation* of cold, or even when there is no cold but the person is frightened. Despite the fact that the chilling stimulus then is intangible, symbolic, or imaginary, it may still call forth a bodily adjustment that normally protects against cold. To elicit such shivering and cutaneous vasoconstriction, sensory impulses—sounds, sights, or odors, for example—that tell of the frightening event must be routed through circuitry in the forebrain, that is, through nervous connections that interpret life experiences. The shivering and vasoconstrictor response are ordered from this level. This bodily maneuver, although effective as protection against actual cold, is inappropriate when a person is simply frightened.

A vivid example of vasoconstriction occurring in association with an intense emotional reaction, but not necessarily accompanied by fear, was encountered during an investigation of subjects with Raynaud's syndrome, a condition characterized by cold hands due to reduction of blood circulation (Mittleman and Wolff 1939). The subjects were required to read a ghoulish account of automobile accidents entitled *And Sudden Death* by J. C. Furnas. Most subjects developed cold hands when they read the article, although one attractive seventeen-year-old girl responded to the story with only a modest fall in her finger temperature. Accordingly, she was asked to read what was considered to be a neutral piece of literature, President Franklin D. Roosevelt's speech dedicating the Jersey City Medical Center. As she read this address her hands became icy cold (see figure 17). The puzzled investigators ascertained that this girl had been at the impressionable age of eleven when Roosevelt was elected president. Her father and brothers had been out of work and there had been no meat on the table. After the election, her father and brothers found work and the family finances suddenly improved. She gave credit to the presi-

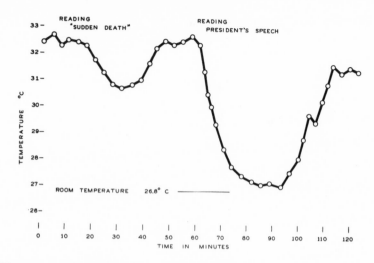

Figure 17. Precipitous fall in finger temperature during an emotionally stressful experience

dent for their good fortune and felt an intense sense of gratitude to him. Perversely, at the next election her father and brothers campaigned vigorously against President Roosevelt and in favor of the Republicans. When occasionally at dinner they said uncomplimentary things about Mr. Roosevelt, the girl felt such a conflict of loyalties between her father and her beloved president that she often left the table without eating.

Thus, the investigators concluded that although the reading of the dedication of the Jersey City Medical Center had no intrinsic emotional meaning, it symbolized the continuing conflict of loyalties so important to the girl. By contrast, the emotional impact of *And Sudden Death* was modest indeed to a regular reader of the *New York Daily News*.

Convincing evidence of the power of the nervous system over the rest of the body may be adduced from our everyday experience and without the artifacts of laboratory experimentation. Such is the case when the stimulus is a symbol which has no intrinsic force of its own but which undergoes interpretation by the brain and thereby gains its power. As already suggested, the rates of secretion of both saliva and gastric juice are closely tied to the experience of emotionally significant events, events that have no conscious or obvious connection with eating. Indeed, the flow of saliva and gastric juice may cease altogether during sudden fright or flow profusely when an individual is frustrated and hostile but quite without appetite.

Among commonly encountered cardiovascular disturbances is a reaction appropriate to running or other vigorous exercise requiring that more blood be delivered to the muscles. This is accomplished through an increase in heart rate and cardiac output and a lowering of peripheral resistance. Precisely the same bodily reaction occurs in the man who is driving his automobile and suddenly hears the shrill whir of a motorcycle policeman's siren. He is not running or even planning to run, if he is wise, and yet his cardiovascular apparatus behaves as if he were running, and as if his muscles needed added nourishment.

Some of the brain circuitry involved in anticipatory adaptations or "as if" reactions was identified by Robert Rushmer and his associates (Rushmer and Smith 1959). Through electrical stimulation of the brain, they were able to produce in dogs the hemodynamic changes of exercise without the animals' engaging in any movement whatever.

Myriad circumstances encountered in our daily lives are capable of triggering visceral reactions. Hearing words which impart good news or bad, seeing a frightening sight, smelling a reminiscent odor, or taking into the mouth a substance with a disgusting taste may provide appropriate input for a variety of complex effector (motor) activities in the body. Nausea, with accompanying changes in motor activity of the stomach and duodenum, can be produced not only by emetic drugs and vestibular stimulation but also by a discussion of emotionally sensitive topics (Wolf 1965a). Some years ago I showed that nausea is always accompanied by interruption of gastric motor activity, loss of gastric tonus, and usually a transitory increase in the contractile state of the duodenum. The nauseating effect of a discussion of sensitive topics was demonstrated in a female who was engaged in a conversation about possible pregnancy. Almost immediately there occurred a sudden cessation of vigorous waves of gastric motor activity, a transitory increase in the contractile state of the duodenum, and nausea. This condition might be called hyperemesis gravidarum praecox, because the young woman was not pregnant at the time. The mere discussion of the pregnancy made her ill. In another experiment with a hospitalized soldier during the New Guinea campaign in World War II, it was possible to observe, fluoroscopically, complete cessation of gastric movements with accompanying nausea simply by initiating a discussion of lurking Japanese or the horrors of the jungle (Wolf 1947).

In collaborative studies involving a good many investigators, "as if" reactions were documented in nearly all of the bodily organ systems: the skin (Graham and Wolf 1950 and 1953; Wolff, Lorenz, and Graham 1951), the bronchi (Holmes et al. 1950), the esophagus (Wolf and Almy 1949), the stomach (Wolf and Wolff 1942), the heart (Wolf and Goodell 1968), the blood vessels (Wolf et al. 1955), the bladder (Straub, Ripley, and Wolf 1949a and 1949b), the uterus and the vagina (Duncan and Taylor 1952), and the metabolic mechanisms expressed as diabetes (Hinkle and Wolf 1950 and 1952). In each instance the patterned responses observed were appropriate to a particular adaptive function but had been inappropriately invoked in response to life situations that were threatening or adverse in some fashion. In some instances, there were potentially damaging tissue changes as well. Since the experiments were necessarily brief, however, a link to long-term disturbances and structural changes could only be inferred. Nevertheless, we were able to catch a glimpse of the intermediary mechanisms that make possible the impact of psychological and social forces on the processes of health and disease.

One of the most vivid examples, and one involving an organ that is easily accessible to view, grew out of studies on the nose undertaken by Thomas Holmes, Helen Goodell, Harold Wolff, and me (1950). The most obvious use for the nose is to smell. Odors are among numerous organic molecules that trig-

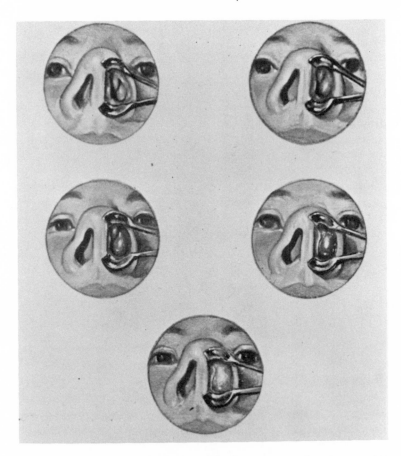

Figure 18. A view into the cavity of the human nose showing varying degrees of swelling of the septum and turbinates

ger a great variety of behaviors. Indeed, smelling is basic to the adjustment of most vertebrates and especially mammals. It seems almost vestigial in man, although even in him certain odors will elicit vital protective reactions and other behaviors. "Air conditioning," the process of warming and moistening inspired air and filtering it to some degree so that it is in a suitable state to encounter the delicate alveolar surfaces of the lungs, is an important function of the nose, and for man probably the most important. When inspired air is contaminated by noxious substances such as smoke, or the fumes of certain chemicals, the nose can provide some protection through swelling of the turbinates and an increase in the flow of mucus.

Holmes and his collaborators were able to elicit the "air conditioning" response experimentally by exposing a person to a series of noxious stimuli, first tangible and directed against the airways, then in the form of pain, and finally delivered as symbols.

Inhalation for one minute of ammonium carbonate fumes provoked sudden hyperemia (engorgement) and swelling of the nasal structures with hypersecretion and obstruction. Associated with these nasal changes there occurred lacrimation

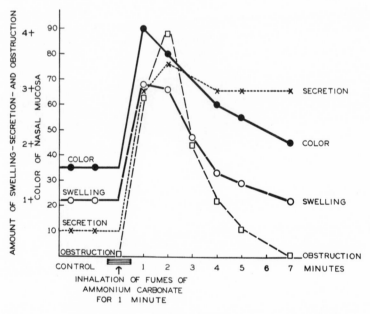

Figure 19. Changes in nasal function following the inhalation of ammonium carbonate

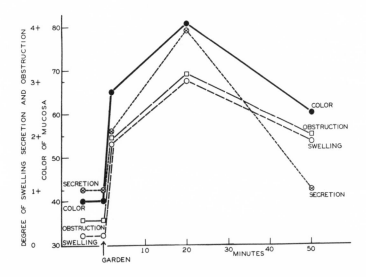

Figure 20. Nasal changes during an acute attack of "hay fever"

and spasm of the eyelids, as well as strenuous coughing. This is an example of an appropriate, though perhaps exaggerated, protective reaction on the part of the organism, an effort at shutting out, washing away, neutralizing, and ejecting an offending substance.

Another type of tangible assault directed against the airways is the inhalation of pollens to which a person may be sensitive. Accordingly, a subject was studied in an attack of hay fever. Prior to the attack, the subject's septum and turbinates were comparatively pale and appeared normal. Immediately upon beginning to cut flowers in his garden, however, he began to weep and sneeze. His membranes had become engorged with blood, wet, and swollen.

This particular attack was an abortive one, but we frequently observed that when the swelling of the membranes was sustained, the engorgement subsided, leaving the membranes pale but still swollen. This pale, swollen state is the usual appearance of the nose of the hay fever sufferer when he arrives at the doctor's office for treatment. It would appear,

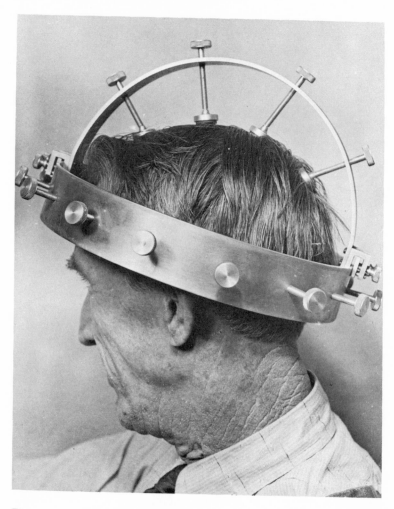

Figure 21. Constricting headband used for the experimental production of headache

however, that as in the case of inhalation of irritating fumes, the engorgement comes first, thus providing another instance in which the protective bodily reaction of shutting out and washing away may be invoked.

The next step in the nasal experiments was to inflict upon a subject a nonspecific threat, not directed at his respiratory passages. Accordingly, the subject's head was constricted in a tight-fitting steel crown which gave rise to an intense headache. This was a highly unpleasant experience for him, associated with feelings of apprehension, and he developed the same protective reaction as that described above for tangible stimuli to the nose.

The final aim of the study was to learn whether or not symbolic threats which did not involve the application of physical trauma could induce such a protective pattern of nasal changes. A sufferer from chronic vasomotor rhinitis (hay fever) whose nasal structures at the time of observation were normal was forcibly reminded that he was caught in the toils of an unfavorable marriage, that his wife was using him for a meal ticket and giving him nothing in return. He promptly began to display the evidences of nasal hyperfunctioning

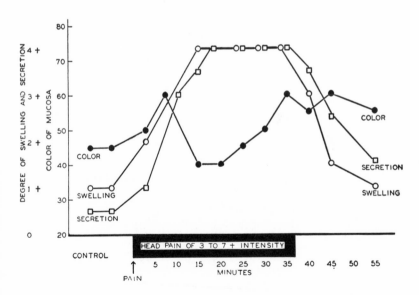

Figure 22. Nasal changes during painful compression of head

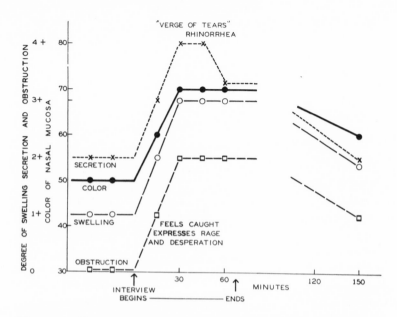

Figure 23. Changes in nasal function induced by a stressful interview

noted above and there was an almost complete obstruction of his breathing. He described himself as being on the verge of tears, although he did not actually weep. After this discussion was ended, the subject was reassured and diverted, and an hour later his nasal functions had returned toward normal.

In other experiments, the contribution of psychological factors to the effect of ragweed pollen in inducing an attack of hayfever or asthma was explored (Treuting and Ripley 1948). Whether or not attacks occurred in pollen-sensitive subjects exposed to controlled amounts of pollen circulated in the laboratory without their knowledge depended in large part on the emotional state of the individual. By manipulating a discussion with the patient, the investigators were able either to block an attack or to induce one, even in the absence of pollen. Clearly, this demonstrated an "as if" reaction.

Several years ago Harold Wolff and I had the opportunity to

study the bodily effects of symbols—i.e., emotionally significant events—in Tom, an otherwise healthy man who had an
opening in his abdominal wall more than an inch in diameter
that led directly into his stomach (Wolf and Wolff 1942). This
opening was the result of a surgical operation required forty-
five years earlier because of a stricture of the esophagus in-
curred when Tom swallowed scalding hot clam chowder. In
experimental studies, it was possible to actually measure the
response of Tom's stomach to meaningful events in his life.
When Tom was angry or resentful, the lining of his stomach
would become suffused with blood, acid gastric juice would
well up, and the contractions of his stomach would intensify,
a behavior characteristic of the stomach in preparation for
digestion. But when Tom was frightened or depressed, his
stomach would pale and secretion and motor activity would
cease, often as a prelude to nausea, a pattern that would be
appropriately protective after the ingestion of poisons.

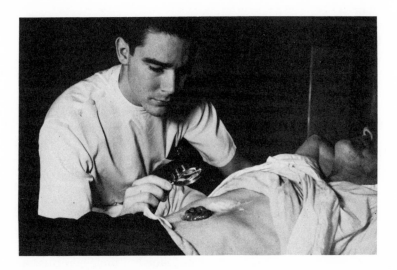

Figure 24. The author with the fistulous subject, Tom, during the
early period of the studies

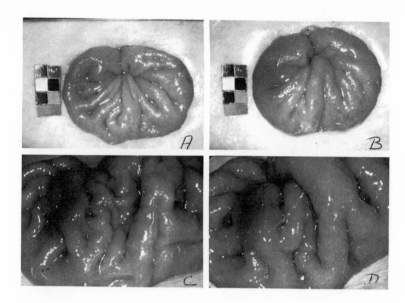

Figure 25.
a. Tom's gastric mucosa under average circumstances
b. The hyperemic engorged mucosa associated with gastric hyperfunction. Note hemorrhagic spots indicating increased fragility of the turgid membrane. The checker pattern indicates uniformity of photographic technique.
c. Close-up of (a) with interior folds exposed by increased intraabdominal pressure
d. Same type of close-up of (b). Note merger of slender folds in hyperfunctioning stomach.

Placebo Effects

Our studies of Tom yielded the first objective demonstration of tangible, measurable effects of placebo administration (Wolf 1959a). Although for many years the favorable effects of placebos (inert materials) had been thought to be imaginary, we sometimes found striking changes following their administration, changes that mimicked or even exceeded the effects of powerful drugs. Under some circumstances, placebos would counteract or cancel out the effects of powerful drugs. We learned that potent drugs could also act as placebos, with their placebo action either reinforcing or counteracting the usual effect of the drug. Experiments in other subjects showed, for example, that the usual nauseating effects of syrup of ipecac could be altogether obliterated by the "placebo effects" of the drug. As already noted, nausea, however induced, is associated with interruption of contractile activity and relaxation of the wall of the stomach. Nausea was induced in a twenty-eight-year-old woman by introducing 10 cc of syrup of ipecac into her stomach through a tube which was also connected to a device that could record the stomach's contractions. On a second occasion she came to the laboratory suffering from the nausea and vomiting of pregnancy. Again the tube was introduced into her stomach. After a suitable control period, 10 cc of syrup of ipecac, the same dose as before, was injected

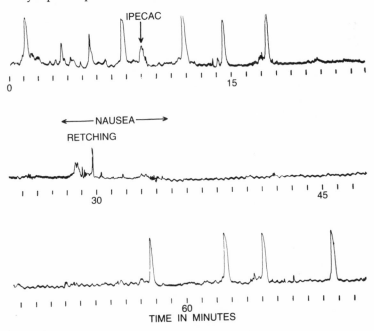

Figure 26. Interruption of stomach contractions followed by nausea, both induced by ipecac

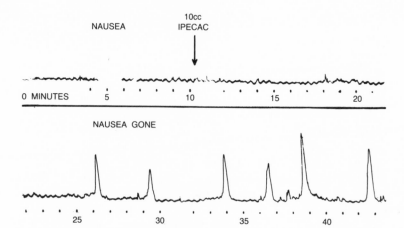

Figure 27. The placebo properties of ipecac here exceed its nauseating properties, as the same dose used in figure 26 is followed by disappearance of nausea and resumption of stomach contractions.

through the tube. She was told, however, that she was being given medicine that would abolish her nausea. Within twenty minutes the nausea had subsided completely and did not recur until the following morning. Coincident with the disappearance of nausea normal contractile activity was recorded, as shown in figure 27.

In a related study, eighteen medical students acted as subjects for an experiment designed to test the effects of placebos (Wolf 1959b). They were given an identical lactose placebo on two occasions by two different experimenters. In response to placebo administration by one of the experimenters, each of the subjects increased his gastric acid secretion, while placebos administered by the other investigator caused a decrease in gastric secretion in each case.

It is evident from such findings that placebo effects may be either favorable or unfavorable. In fact, some years ago we observed in several individuals "toxic" effects following administration of placebos, including skin rash, vomiting and diarrhea, and sudden fall in blood pressure with fainting (Wolf and Pinksy 1954).

It has been suggested that the ability of acupuncture to mitigate pain or to lessen a variety of other symptoms may be due in large part to its placebo effect, although the possibility remains that, as proposed by its advocates, acupuncture may activate as yet unidentified inhibitory neural interactions in the brain and spinal cord. It is also possible that, as suggested in the case of placebos, acupuncture may evoke the production of enkephalins capable of modulating afferent traffic in pain nerves (Levine, Gordon, and Fields 1978). The American practice of employing needle puncture to administer vitamin B_{12} has proved to be a widely used and often effective placebo. A fanciful comparison of such Western needlework with acupuncture is shown in figure 28. Significantly, the Chinese physician's healing powers are such that it is unnecessary for him to inject vitamin B_{12} through his needle. Other procedures

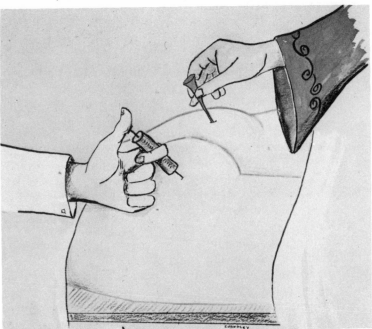

Figure 28. Needlework by the ancient Chinese physician and the modern American doctor

that may have powerful placebo effects in addition to presumed specific actions include biofeedback, autogenic training, transcendental meditation, progressive relaxation, guided imagery, hypnotic suggestion, and yoga. Even surgery has its placebo aspect. Indeed the encouragement offered and the optimistic conviction engendered by any therapeutic attempt may play its part in the healing process.

BEHAVIORAL TECHNIQUES

The behavioral procedures mentioned above have been used as treatments for a wide range of conditions characterized by disturbances of autonomic function. Among these disorders are migraine headaches, asthma, skin disorders, and high blood pressure. Little is known of the basic mechanisms that underlie the capacity of such methods to influence bodily processes or that distinguish the effects of one of them from those of another. A much more extensively studied method is Pavlovian conditioning, whereby it is possible to order the behavior of certain viscera as well as skeletal muscles. The procedure involves the repeated coupling of a stimulus that would normally elicit the function with a symbol such as a sound, sight, or odor, so that eventually even perceiving the symbol will cause the subject to respond in anticipation of the ordinarily appropriate "unconditioned" stimulus. In contrast, operant or instrumental conditioning achieves its effects through the repeated association of a particular behavior with either rewards or punishments. Rewards and punishments successfully applied to human subjects have consisted mainly of evidences of social approval or disapproval.

A wide variety of bodily effects have been attributed to the various maneuvers described above, including the elicitation, modification, or inhibition of immunologic, metabolic, and vascular functions that adapt an individual to his environment. Such behavioral techniques are designed to establish new habits of visceral or skeletal muscle behavior by tapping the motivational power of social relationships and of individual attitudes, aspirations, and beliefs. It remains to ascertain precisely how these measures work.

4. Control of Adaptive Behavior

The Circuitry between Stimulus and Response

The task of identifying intermediary mechanisms between stimulus and response was begun one hundred years ago when B. Danilewski showed that the behavior of internal organs could be modified by electrical stimulation of the frontal lobes of the brain (Danilewski 1875). Like most entirely original observations, his discovery was disbelieved, criticized, and ultimately ignored. More recently, however, and thanks to the work of such investigators as Orville Smith of the University of Washington, his work has found ample confirmation (Smith, Stephenson, and Randall 1974; Smith et al. 1979). Modern workers, in fact, are beginning to map in the brain the connections between life experiences and the functioning of bodily organs. The perception and evaluation of life experiences is accomplished in the frontal lobes of the brain. From here signals that affect the tissues of the body are transmitted by nerve connections to control centers in the brain stem and spinal cord that ordinarily subserve simple protective reflexes but are also subject to excitation or inhibition from the forebrain circuits involved in the interpretation of life experience. Other pathways involve the activation of circulating substances, including hormones. Thus, almost any bodily response may be called into play as part of an individual's attempt to adjust to people and circumstances about him.

The business of the vastly versatile nervous system of man is carried on by a wondrous series of electronic and chemical events that take place in and among the cells of the brain and spinal cord. Each nerve cell, or neuron, consists of a cell body where the nucleus is lodged and where most but not all of the intracellular chemical transformations take place. Some transformations occur in multiple processes called dendrites, which bring information to the cell body from connections with other nerves, and ultimately in an extension of the nerve cell called the axon, which branches many times to convey information to neurons nearby or even at a great distance. The neuron is enveloped in a double layered membrane which selectively allows ingress and egress of substances concerned with the nutrition of the cell, the manufacture of its products, and their delivery. Within the neuron, fluid nutrients and metabolic products travel in all directions, producing the so-called axoplasmic flow. Neurons communicate with one another via synapses. A synapse is where parts of two nerve cells are brought together in close apposition but with a gap, the synaptic cleft, in between. The activation of one nerve cell by another takes place by virtue of a small amount of chemical substance, a neurotransmitter, being ejected at the synapse by one nerve. The neurotransmitter travels across the short distance of the synaptic cleft to receptors on the surface membrane of another nerve, thus causing the second nerve to fire. The firing consists of a depolarization of the electrical charges lined up along the length of the nerve, positive on the outer surface of the membrane, and negative on the inner. If a further connection is required, the second nerve extrudes neurotransmitter at a further synapse, and so on until the business at hand is accomplished. After firing, a neuron repolarizes, recovering the opposing array of electrical charges along the course of its membrane.

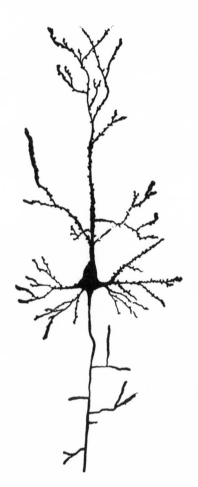

Neurotransmitters, synthesized within the nerve cells and transported along the axon, may be inhibitory as well as excitatory, thereby enabling one neuron to block the discharge of another that would otherwise be stimulated to fire by excitatory synaptic connections with a third neuron. The inhibitory neurotransmitter "freezes" the polarization of the membrane of the second neuron, creating what is called a hyperpolarized state, in which the neuron is immune to the stimulating effects of its connection with the third neuron and is hence, for the time being, incapable of firing.

Such inhibitory influences may be exerted on either side of a synapse, either blocking the release of excitatory neurotransmitter by the initial stimulating neuron or blocking its effect by preventing depolarization of the recipient neuron. The cells of the nervous system are subject to influence not only by way of their synaptic connections, but are controlled to some extent by more direct communications from adjacent cells as well as by circulating molecules, including hormones, nutrients, and metabolic products, and by the surrounding temperature and degree of

Figure 29. A highly developed neuron

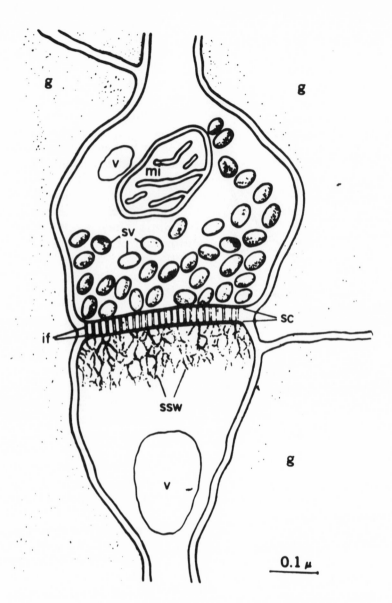

Figure 30. A diagrammatic representation of a synapse. Letters refer to organelles (microscopic structures).

acidity. Cell-to-cell messages are communicated by way of electrically charged ions and organic chemicals that interact with specialized receptors on the surface of the cell membranes within the nervous system. Thereby are implemented the regulatory strategies that control the behavior of all the tissues of the body.

In addition to its neuronal network, the nervous system contains vast numbers of glial cells, formerly thought to function primarily as a supporting lattice, but recently discovered to contribute substantially to biosynthetic and regulatory functions. Those glia that are located adjacent to synapses help to clear the cleft of secreted neurotransmitters by reabsorbing them. Thereby the glia appear to modulate to some extent the traffic of neuronal impulses.

A single neuron in the brains of mammals, including man, may participate in many thousands of synapses. Thus a vast number of interactions, reflecting myriad contingencies, may contribute to the resultant behavior.

INSTINCT AND INTELLIGENCE

The difference between instinct and intelligence depends in part on quantitative considerations, that is, the number of potentially intervening nerve connections between stimulus and response. For example, the behavior of invertebrates low on the evolutionary scale is, for the most part, quite accurately predictable. The "instinctive" nature of their responses to various stimuli is explained by the fact that there is a simple unbranched reflex pathway between stimulus and response. In other words, the synapses that transmit the signals from afferent (sensory) neurons to activate effector (motor) fibers have few if any connections with other neurons that could preempt, inhibit, or otherwise modify the transfer of information.

In contrast, the reflexes of more elaborately developed brains of "higher" animals, including mammals, are subject to modification by a variety of influences from other parts of the brain that also interpret experience. The nature and intensity of a response may be determined not only by the original stimulus but by a host of intervening contingencies. Even responses dependent on the convergence of fairly complex circuitry tend to become habitual. For instance, mammals with relatively sophisticated brains, such as dogs, easily fall into habit patterns, the very predictability of which made possible the brilliant researches of Ivan Pavlov (1927). Nevertheless, under intense emotional stimulation as occurred during the flood in Pavlov's laboratory, modifying circuits came into play and the predictability of his dogs' conditioned responses was lost (1928). As in the case of placebos, identical stimuli may elicit quite different behavioral responses in the same animal under different circumstances, thanks to the complex organization of his nervous system which allows for many influences to interact and thereby determine the nature of a response.

Human behavior results from a highly complex interplay of facilitatory and inhibitory connections which serve the myriad contingencies that, either consciously or unconsciously, govern our decision-making processes. Consequently, human behavior can become predictable only when cues from a number of sources are recognized, understood, and monitored. Modification of responses may be dictated by associations with past experience and may be further modified by attitudes, beliefs, and a multitude of interpersonal vibrations. As already pointed out, the mechanisms whereby the effects of such intangible forces are transmitted and interpreted are still only partly understood.

The operation of the circuits of the central nervous system is often compared to that of a sophisticated computer. There are similarities, but the number of nerve cells and of cell connections (synapses) is vastly greater in the brain than are the connecting electrical circuits in the most advanced computer. As a result, when making decisions that depend on the interplay of multiple forces, the brain is able to deal with many more contingencies than a computer can. Figure 31 suggests the connections required in the brain to process incoming information and to order responses involving internal organs as well as skeletal muscles. While the neurons involved in induc-

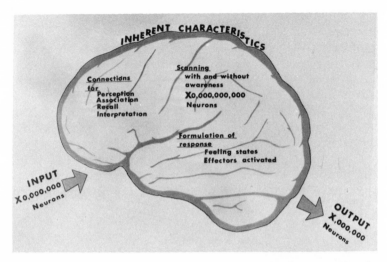

Figure 31. Factors involved in the processing of information by the highest levels of the central nervous system

ing behavior number in the millions, those required to bring information of all sorts to the brain are numbered in the tens of millions. Furthermore, the neurons in the vast multisynaptic network that processes all the information and makes decisions are numbered in the tens of billions.

REGULATION THROUGH INHIBITION

Inhibitory effects, as pointed out above, depend on the elaboration of neurotransmitters that hyperpolarize a neuron and block its firing. Inhibitory pathways in the central nervous system have recently come under increasing scrutiny. Much has been learned through the study of such inhibitory neurotransmitters as glycine and GABA. The latter has been identified not only in association with the cerebellum's Purkinje cells, a major source of inhibitory activity in the brain, but elsewhere in the central nervous system as well, and even peripherally in the walls of arteries and arterioles. Indeed, the nervous system is now known to contain an elaborate inhibitory network that modulates both visceral behavior and the functions of skeletal muscles (Wolf 1970).

Inhibition may be brought to bear in sensory circuits as well as motor circuits, as was demonstrated in a classical experiment illustrated in figure 32 (Hernandez-Peon, Sherrer, and Jouvet 1956). R. Hernandez-Peon and his associates impaled the cochlear nucleus of a cat with a recording electrode. The cochlear nucleus contains synapses between neurons of the auditory nerve as it transmits electrical signals set up by vibrations of the eardrum to neurons that carry the information into the brain, to be interpreted as sounds. The investigators placed a metronome close to the ear of the cat so that with

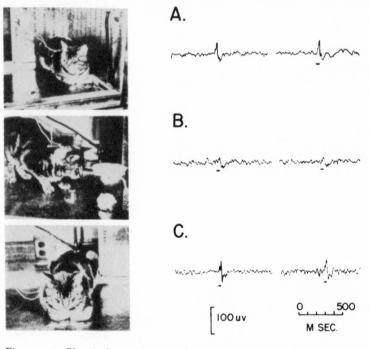

Figure 32. Classical experiment of Hernandez-Peon:
a. Cochlear response during ticking of metronome
b. Interruption of response while cat attends mouse
c. Resumption of cochlear response after removal of mouse

each click of the instrument they were able to record an action potential, reflecting synaptic transmission in the cochlear nucleus. While recording the action potential in synchrony with the click of the metronome, they suddenly brought a mouse into the cat's field of vision. At once the action potential was suppressed, and the electrode signal was dampened, despite the continued clicking of the metronome. As soon as the mouse was removed, the action potential was again recorded. The cat's interest in the mouse had elicited an inhibitory response that temporarily blocked the cat's awareness of the less interesting metronome. A similar mechanism may be in operation when a husband, absorbed in the sports page, fails to hear his wife's request to carry out the garbage. Many other examples of inhibitory activity in sensory circuits have come to light in recent years, notably those that modulate the experience of pain. Inhibition of incoming traffic along pain nerves has been identified at several levels of the spinal cord and brain. Among the neurotransmitters that serve the inhibitory systems are the morphine-like enkephalins and endorphins which play a major role in modulating pain (Van Ree and Terenius 1978).

A vast amount of inhibitory modulation is to be found on the effector, or motor, side of the nervous system as well. Many of the inhibitory neurons are carried in the corticospinal tract in the spinal cord. When there is damage to the corticospinal tract, knee jerks and other tendon reflexes are exaggerated. Movements of the limbs become stiff and awkward. Intact inhibitory pathways originating in the cerebellum, red nucleus, and basal ganglia of the brain are essential to the graceful movements of a ballerina or a champion athlete. Rich interconnections between somatic sensory, visceral sensory, and effector neurons of all sorts have been discovered that link many zones of the central nervous system, including the thalamus, hypothalamus, and limbic cortex, with the frontal lobes.

As more and more has been learned about facilitatory and inhibitory regulation of synaptic transmission at every level of the nervous system, the concept of the reflex nature of bodily regulation has given way to a concept of neural interaction in

which virtually all parts of the nervous system are intercon-
nected so that local perturbations may have widespread effects. In fact, Sir Charles Sherrington, often called the father of
neurophysiology, is said to have stated at the age of eighty
that the study of reflexes had run its course and that efforts
must now be directed to the study of widespread connections
that modify reflex behavior. Pursuit of such studies has clearly
revealed that the somatic and visceral pathways are not two
systems after all but a single system in a state of continuous
dynamic interaction as behaviors are initiated, maintained,
and modified.

Sherrington's remarks about the importance of interconnect-
ing regulators of reflex behaviors have been amply supported
by recent investigations, especially those concerned with circumstances in which protective reflex activities come in conflict with one another. To illustrate, muscular exercise ordinarily requires a dilatation of the arteries of the limbs in order to
supply them with the added nourishment required for the effort. When an individual is in a situation that allows him to
overbreathe to oxygenate the extra quantity of blood going to
the muscles, the required expansion of the blood vessels occurs automatically, thanks to a well-established reflex mechanism. But when he engages in vigorous muscular activity underwater, while holding his breath, the need for oxygen
conservation takes precedence and the "dive reflex" described on page 67 takes over, inhibiting the dilatation of arteries, and requiring that the muscular exercise be accomplished by way of anaerobic (oxygen-free) metabolism
(Bergman, Campbell, and Wildenthal 1972).

Further evidence of regulatory circuits in the brain that
modulate competing reflexes has been provided by G. L. Gebber and L. R. Klevans (1972), who studied the complex circuitry responsible for coordinating the control of arterial pressure with heart rate. Recently acquired knowledge of certain
regulatory molecules (peptides) has taught us that virtually
every bodily adjustment is subject to control or modulation by
a convergence of excitatory and inhibitory chemical influences

exerted by fragments cleaved from larger molecules located throughout the body but especially in the brain, pituitary gland, gastrointestinal tract, liver, and kidney. The cleavage is often the result of a cascade of chemical transformations initiated by nerve impulses. For example, beta lipotropin, a large molecule identified in the pituitary gland, appeared to have no physiological function until less than ten years ago when it was learned that natural cleavage of the molecule under certain circumstances produces highly potent regulatory peptides (endorphins). Attention was first drawn to these substances because of their opium-like properties. Later it was learned that their activities include effects on the contraction of muscular organs, the regulation of body temperature, sugar metabolism, and eating behavior. They also have striking mental effects on motivation, learning, and memory processes. Large doses have induced effects resembling the manifestations of schizophrenia (Rossier et al. 1980)

It is evident from these and other findings that the regulation of behaviors of all sorts requires a balance of excitatory and inhibitory influences. This principle, reminiscent of the ancient Chinese concepts of Yin and Yang, is applicable to all aspects of human behavior. Behavior involving viscera as well as skeletal muscles must be modulated and damped to some extent in order to be maximally adaptive.

BODILY CHANGES—SYMPTOMS AND DISEASE

The rapidly growing understanding of the importance of modulation of all bodily functions arouses the speculation that failure of restraints, or a defective balance between excitatory and inhibitory mechanisms, may be responsible for a broad range of disorders, encompassing, for example, pathological aggressiveness, alcoholism, and epilepsy; visceral disturbances such as the almost ceaseless gastric secretion of hydrochloric acid and protein-splitting enzymes characteristic of duodenal ulcer, the sustained contraction of initially normal arterioles in hypertension, or the exaggerated ratio of destruction of red blood cells in hemolytic anemia; and aberrations in other bodily systems such as the cardiac arrhythmias that lead to sudden death.

Currently available evidence indicates that, for the most part, fatal ventricular arrhythmias associated with myocardial infarction or other cardiac injury are triggered through medullary pathways that connect with brainstem and hypothalamic structures (Schwartz et al. 1978). These same pathways are available to impulses from the frontal lobes and, therefore, may be activated as part of a response to all sorts of circumstances, including emotionally stressful experiences. The orderly sequence of depolarization that is responsible for the normal rhythm of the heart is subject to influence via nervous stimuli as well as via circulating chemical regulators. Thus, stimuli outside of the heart itself may induce the whole range of heartbeat disorders (Wolf 1978).

Fatal ventricular fibrillation has been induced in animals not only by stimulation of either the sympathetic or vagal nerve trunks but also by localized electrical stimulation in many brain areas, including the frontal lobes (Hall, Livingston, and Bloor 1977).

Several investigators have reported the occurrence of cardiac arrhythmias during emotional stress (Katz, Winston, and Megibow 1947; Stevenson et al. 1949; Harvey and Levine 1952). My colleagues and I have been able to observe in an experimental setting serious disturbances in the orderly process of contraction of the chambers of the heart, induced in presumably healthy subjects by a discussion of emotionally stressful topics (figure 33). Abnormalities reflected in the electrocardiogram as grave disturbances in the rhythm of the heartbeat with consequent impairment of perfusion of the heart muscle itself were observed during intense emotional stress in subjects in whom no structural cardiac disease could be demonstrated. There is emerging evidence that some of the electrocardiographic changes, including those that may be characteristic of myocardial infarction (heart attack), may be the result of neurally-mediated coronary vascular constriction

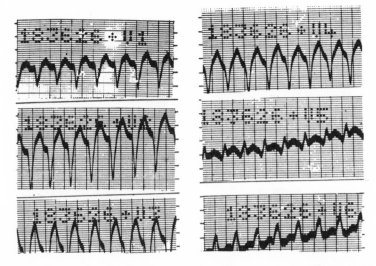

Figure 33. Ventricular fibrillation induced by an emotionally stressful interview in an apparently healthy young man. Prior to and following the interview the electrocardiogram was normal.

perhaps with associated increased oxygen demand (Maseri et al. 1978; Hellstrom 1979).

A vividly illustrative case was that of a fifty-four-year-old business executive who, on the occasion of a routine annual physical checkup, was told to come in prepared for a sigmoidoscopic examination (inspection of the lower bowel through a rigid lighted tube). His first test that day was an electrocardiogram, which surprisingly revealed fresh evidence of local oxygen deprivation in the heart muscle, a condition known as inferior ischaemia. The patient was transported at once to the hospital, where in the coronary care unit a new electrocardiogram proved to be entirely normal. At this point the patient acknowledged that he had anticipated the sigmoidoscopic examination with anxiety amounting to dread, an emotional state reflected in his heart by a vigorous constriction of one of the coronary artery branches, thus temporarily depriving a portion of the heart muscle of its normal oxygen supply. Such

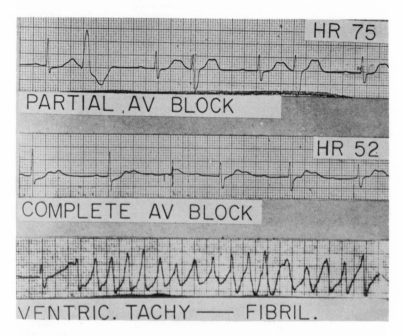

Figure 34. A series of conduction defects and arrhythmias requiring emergency treatment observed following severe emotional stress. Before and after the episode, the electrocardiogram of this otherwise healthy woman was normal.

"ischaemic episodes" frequently progress to frank myocardial infarction.

Myocardial infarction, in turn, may give rise through reflex pathways to fatal arrhythmia. But potentially fatal arrhythmias may also be induced in the absence of myocardial infarction and without reflex stimulation as a result of neural processes in the higher centers of the brain actuated by troublesome life experiences. Indeed, sudden death in humans (presumably arrhythmic) has been noted under circumstances of sudden fright, social exclusion, and emotional depression, the so-called "giving-up" death discussed by G. L. Engel (1978). Sudden death under circumstances of intense emotional stress was reported nearly one hundred years ago by L. Feigel (1887), and doubtless there were earlier instances noted. J. Bruhn and collaborators, in a prospective study of patients who had sustained a myocardial infarction in the past, were able to predict with fair accuracy on the basis of psychological measures which of the group of sixty-seven subjects would die suddenly during a follow-up period of ten years (Bruhn et al. 1974).

Psychological forces appear to contribute to disease processes by introducing bias into normal visceral regulatory mechanisms, a bias that might result from disturbed receptor or effector activity or from disordered modulation by inhibitory or feedback circuits. Neither overt emotional display nor conscious awareness of emotional conflict is required for meaningful life situations to produce such disturbances.

"LEARNED" CONTROL OF VISCERAL FUNCTION

It has already been pointed out that the success of behavioral techniques such as operant (instrumental) conditioning requires the introduction of a reward or punishment that is usually based on social approval or disapproval. Other techniques, loosely grouped under the term "biofeedback," involve a common principle, namely, transmitting to the subject a signal that indicates whether or not he is succeeding in manipulating the measured function in the desired direction and to the desired degree.

Still other methods—autogenic training, meditation, and progressive relaxation, to name a few—exploit a biological characteristic long familiar to the yogis of India. Through the use of these various techniques, therapeutic effects have been achieved in attempts to correct cardiac rate and rhythm, arterial blood pressure level, gastric acid secretion, and esophageal and rectal sphincter action.

Hypnosis is another device whereby regulatory neural circuits may be recruited to control the behavior of vascular, glandular, and other bodily structures. In the mid-1870s, Wilhelm Wundt made observations on hypnosis and developed what is now called psychophysiology (Wundt 1872). Wundt owed his introduction to hypnosis to Charles Richet. Richet,

Above left: Figure 35. Wilhelm Wundt. *Above right:* Figure 36. Charles Richet. *Left:* Figure 37. Jean Louis Martin Charcot. (Photos courtesy of National Library of Medicine)

as an intern at one of the hospitals in Paris, had a patient, a sixteen-year-old girl, with a hysterical illness. In his published paper, which is delightful, the first four pages are taken up with his apology for undertaking any such thing as hypnosis, excusing it on the grounds of his curiosity and acknowledging at the same time that necromancy is very bad business (Richet 1881). Richet repeatedly hypnotized the girl and thus eliminated her symptoms, but they eventually recurred after each hypnosis. As he rotated among the hospitals of Paris, Richet served at the Salpetriere Hospital under the supervision of the world-renowned neurologist Jean Louis Martin Charcot. It was Richet who interested Charcot in the medical and scientific potential of hypnosis. Wundt also learned about Richet's work and systematically studied hypnosis in relation to governing bodily functions; in so doing, he put psychophysiology on the map.

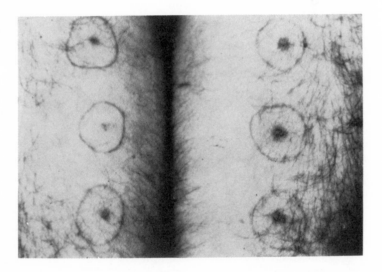

Figure 38. Contrasting reactions to an identical heat stimulus on the two forearms. Hypnotic suggestions were made that the right arm was immune to injury and that the left was extra sensitive. Note the larger areas of tissue destruction on the left.

The effects of hypnosis are apparently achieved through the activation of inhibitory neurons in both sensory and motor pathways. On the sensory side, anesthesia may be induced by a mechanism comparable to that in the experiment of Hernandez-Peon, already described, where concentration on one experience blocked incoming information from another. Tissue damage may also be mitigated or enhanced through the use of hypnosis. Chapman, Goodell, and Wolff (1959) were able by hypnotic suggestions of anesthesia to limit blister formation on one arm from heat applied to the skin. At the same time, they enhanced blister formation on the other arm by suggesting during hypnosis that the skin was sore and highly vulnerable.

Placebo effects provide other examples of the manipulation of bodily responses by psychologic means. Recent evidence suggests that the analgesic effect of placebos in painful conditions may involve the elaboration of endorphins, the body's own morphine-like secretions mentioned above (Levine, Gordon, and Fields 1978).

PATTERNING OF ADAPTIVE RESPONSES

As the character of bodily responses may be determined not only by the intrinsic nature of a stimulus but also by its significance, the responses become, in a sense, goal-directed or purposeful. In short, they may be adaptive or protective. As such they involve discrete afferent and efferent neural circuits in a cooperative response pattern. Even ancient protective behaviors that have persisted over the long course of biological evolution, developing from simple reflexes in primitive invertebrates, have evolved as intricate and elaborate networks that involve many effector pathways in the central nervous system, both somatic and visceral. Such complex response patterns are often coordinated from a single place in the brain, a command site. Some widely-used adaptive patterns include the shift from carbohydrate to fat metabolism in starvation and the vascular and glandular adjustments required to maintain a constant body temperature in the face of a 100°F shift in the temperature of the environment. One of the adaptations most basic to survival is the fascinating "dive reflex," a phylogenetically ancient adaptive mechanism that conserves oxygen.

THE DIVE REFLEX

The principal elements of the dive reflex, elicited simply by immersing the face in water, are listed in figure 39. The phenomenon was discovered nearly a hundred years ago by the French scientist Paul Bert, who was impressed with the length of time ducks held their heads underwater while they fished for food. Although he noted an associated slowing of the heart rates he left the problem there, assuming that an oxygen-storing mechanism enabled the ducks to remain underwater

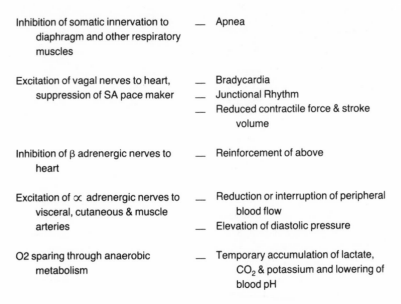

Inhibition of somatic innervation to diaphragm and other respiratory muscles	— Apnea
Excitation of vagal nerves to heart, suppression of SA pace maker	— Bradycardia — Junctional Rhythm — Reduced contractile force & stroke volume
Inhibition of β adrenergic nerves to heart	— Reinforcement of above
Excitation of ∝ adrenergic nerves to visceral, cutaneous & muscle arteries	— Reduction or interruption of peripheral blood flow — Elevation of diastolic pressure
O2 sparing through anaerobic metabolism	— Temporary accumulation of lactate, CO_2 & potassium and lowering of blood pH

Figure 39. Features of the dive reflex

Figure 40. Paul Bert (courtesy of National Library of Medicine)

longer than the air held in their lungs would normally warrant (Bert 1879).

Charles Richet, already referred to, who was professor of physiology in Paris and later winner of a Nobel Prize for the discovery of anaphylaxis (fatal collapse caused by sensitivity to a foreign substance), suspected instead that the ducks were able to invoke a reflex oxygen-conserving mechanism. This he confirmed, in the early 1890s, by a crucial experiment in which he tied off the tracheas of several ducks. Those ducks kept in air died in six or seven minutes, but those whose heads were held underwater survived an average of twenty-one minutes. Richet suggested that contact of the nasal cavities with water somehow set off the reflex by stimulating an afferent branch of the trigeminal nerve (Richet 1894).

Nearly seventy years passed before the final proof of Richet's deduction was established by the studies of Harald T. Andersen of the University of Oslo (1963). In a series of nerve-cutting experiments he documented the fact that the diving reflex, evidenced by slowing of the heart, depended on the integrity of the ophthalmic branch of the trigeminal nerve. With the nerve intact a duck could survive underwater for twenty minutes, but when the branch was severed bilaterally, the heart of the immersed duck failed to slow and the duck survived for only six or seven minutes. The command site for this highly organized protective maneuver that utilizes both somatic pathways (to the skeletal muscles of respiration) and autonomic pathways (to the smooth muscle of the arteries and arterioles and to the pacemaker and conduction apparatus of the heart) is located in a portion of the brainstem called the nucleus of the tractus solitarius (Gunn, Friedman, and Byers 1960).

The command site of the dive reflex is connected to nerve pathways in the forebrain. In company with other usually automatic responses, the reflex is subject to intensification, restraint, or cancellation by signals from higher centers of the brain, especially those that interpret life experience and formulate responses in keeping with prevailing circumstances, including social circumstances. As an example, the porpoise, or dolphin, a mammal with a highly developed dive reflex and also a very advanced brain, displays all the elements of the dive reflex when he immerses his snout to dive, but when he is simply engaging in play, dipping in and out of the water, the dive reflex is totally suppressed.

P. F. Scholander with the help of Baird Hastings showed in an ingenious experiment that fish when out of water (their normal oxygen-supplying environment) display the heart rate slowing characteristic of the dive reflex (Scholander 1962). Flying fish were attached to the leads of an electrocardiogram

Figure 41. Baird Hastings on the deck on the *Alpha Helix*

through the line of a fishing pole. Hastings, holding the fishing pole, clocked the intervals when the flying fish vaulted from the surface of the water. Each period in the air was associated with heart rate slowing. The ancient phylogenetic roots of the oxygen-conserving reflex are further apparent from the study of Pinsker and Feinstein, who demonstrated heart rate slowing in a primitive invertebrate, the aplysia, upon its removal from the water (Feinstein et al. 1977).

The oxygen-conserving reflex is not only an ancient protective device but a predominant one when in competition with other protective-adaptive responses. For example, S. A. Bergman and his associates showed that although the body's usual response during muscular exercise includes a vasodilatation in

Figure 42. Aplysia Californica (from Feinstein et al. 1977)

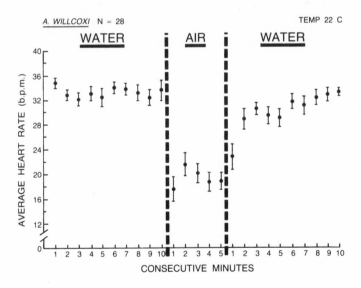

Figure 43. The "reverse" dive reflex elicited in aplysia (from Feinstein et al. 1977)

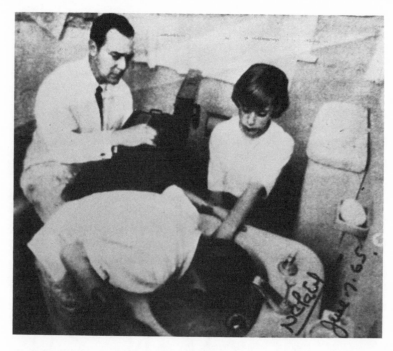

Figure 44. The author and his son eliciting the dive reflex in a wash-basin in Paris

the extremities, vasomotor behavior during vigorous exercise underwater is controlled by the mechanisms of the dive reflex, so that vasoconstriction to the muscles is maintained and exercise is carried out via anaerobic metabolism (Bergman, Campbell, and Wildenthal 1972). Similarly, R. Elsner and B. Gooden (1970) observed that the usual reactive increase in blood supply that follows interruption of circulation to an extremity is markedly reduced when the circulation to an arm is interrupted during immersion of the face in water.

My interest in the dive reflex was stimulated by the work of Scholander. I began to study the phenomenon while I was on sabbatical leave in Paris in 1962–63. I installed an electrocardiograph in the bathroom of our apartment and persuaded the members of my family and what friends I had left to dunk

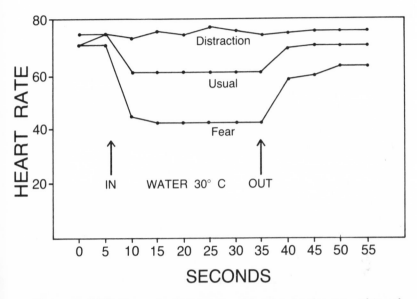

Figure 45. Differences in the degree of heart rate slowing achieved during facial immersion under various emotional states

their faces in the sink filled with water. The striking findings from the study were that heart rate slowing during face immersion was greatly accentuated in the presence of fear, but was totally blocked when the subject was distracted or was concentrating intensely on another matter (Wolf 1965b and 1965c).

The dive reflex is one of a vast repertoire of behaviors that adapt the individual to environmental stresses of all sorts. Each involves discrete patterned responses that are activated and coordinated by the nervous system.

THE LABILE SYSTEM

From the studies of the nose we learned that those most susceptible to rapid and pronounced changes in nasal and bronchial function in response to specific stimuli also displayed a wider variation in the behavior of their respiratory mucous membranes during the course of an ordinary day and also from day to day, suggesting thereby a lack of normal damping or modulation. We then found wide swings in other bodily systems among those susceptible to symptomatic disturbances. An opportunity to make automatic recordings of blood pressure throughout several hours of the day or night made it possible to show that variations from time to time in systolic and diastolic pressure were much greater in individuals with incipient hypertension than in those who did not go on to develop hypertension (Schneider, Costiloe, and Wolf 1971). Moreover, among the hypertensive patients it was possible to induce greater increases in blood pressure by stressful interviews than was possible in subjects without hypertension. Such extreme variability, or lability, in a particular system also characterized individuals in whom we were able to elicit, by psychological stimuli, cutaneous lesions, excessive secretion of acid gastric juice, major deviations in colon motility, and even the precipitation of a migraine headache (Wolf and Goodell 1968).

A striking characteristic of those who suffer periodically from vascular headache is that the amplitude of their extracranial arterial pulsations varies over a wider range, even in headache-free periods, than those of non-headache-prone individuals. The greatest variability in cranial artery behavior can be observed on the days immediately preceding a migraine attack. Other vascular beds, including the smaller vessels of the conjuntiva (the membrane which lines the eyelids) and the nasal mucosae, the arterioles concerned with the regulation of arterial pressure, and the capillaries that participate in maintaining fluid balance, have also been found to display a noteworthy lability of behavior in those with vascular headache (Wolf and Wolff 1953). Whether a deficient damping mechanism is inherent or acquired has not been settled. In any case, whatever modulation exists is achieved by a balance of excitatory and inhibitory activity in the nerve circuits that govern the function in question.

The principal significance of a well-controlled balance of ex-

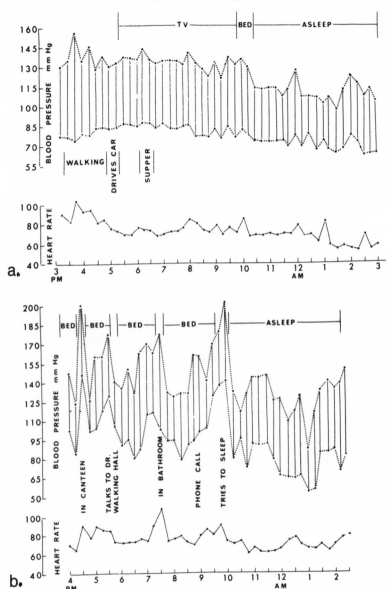

Figure 46. Continuous automatic recording of blood pressure day and night (from Schneider, Costiloe, and Wolf 1971):
a. A healthy subject with frequently stable blood pressure
b. Wide variations in the patient with essential hypertension

Figure 47. The importance of balancing forces (by permission of Bill Mauldin and Wil-Jo Associates, © 1978, courtesy of *Chicago Sun-Times*)

citatory and inhibitory activity is clearly illustrated by the difference between the sound of a player piano activated by a perforated roll of paper, and that of a keyboard under the fingers of a great artist, where the beauty of the music stems in part from modulation of the force applied to the piano keys, modulation that results from the interplay of excitatory and inhibitory volleys of nerve impulses on the muscles of the fingers, hands, and arms of the pianist. For our purposes, not only bad music but much pathological visceral behavior may be a consequence of insufficient balancing restraint. As shown in figure 47, the laws of nature prevail even in public affairs.

When bodily responses involving internal organs are either insufficient or exaggerated, there is created an imbalance with the potential of tissue damage, disability, and even death. Meaningful life situations are capable, in suitably susceptible individuals, of inducing major changes in the behavior of the organs of the human body—changes that resemble those encountered in illness, brought about by nerve connections between the visceral regulatory centers in the brain stem and circuits in the forebrain which interpret life experience and whose activity can preempt the control of reflex and other lower-range mechanisms.

Recent discoveries have established that the inherent characteristics of the brain that determine behavior derive to some extent, at least, from the quantity and distribution of catecholamines and other neurotransmitters. Indeed, there is strong indication that the behavioral aberrations characteristic of manic depressive psychosis and schizophrenia reflect major shifts in the concentration of neurotransmitters in specific areas of the brain (Wolf and Berle 1976). Such discoveries, important as they are in clarifying mechanisms, do not settle the question of what causes these devastating mental illnesses. In bodily diseases as well, it is important not to interpret mechanism as cause. Every process requires a mechanism irrespective of underlying factors that determine susceptibility, precipitating events that trigger the process, or forces that tend to sustain or perpetuate the mechanism. The mechanism itself is not the cause. To understand cause, we must learn more of the human spirit, of individual needs and aspirations. These are presumably defined by the intricate neuronal network of the brain as it plays upon the neurons that regulate the functions of cells, tissues, and organs.

5. The Consequences of Adaptive Behavior: Health and Disease

THE SOCIAL DIMENSION:
INTERDEPENDENCE, COMMUNICATION, AND CONTROL

Having reviewed the evidence that problems arising in the course of human relationships should be counted among the many causal factors of disability and disease, as well as some of the evidence for the mechanisms whereby they exert their effects on the body, let us explore those aspects of human relationships that are conducive to health and, in so doing, emphasize the immense importance of interdependence, good communication, and modulation of behavior.

Rene Dubos, whose work was referred to earlier, has related the quality of interrelationships to health and disease as follows:

> All living things, from man to the smallest microbe, live in association with other living things. Through the phenomena of biological evolution, an equilibrium is established which permits the different components of biological systems to live at peace together, indeed often to help one another. Whenever the equilibrium is disturbed by any means whatever either internal

or external, one of the components of the system is favored at the expense of the other . . . and then come about the processes of disease. [Dubos 1953]

Such a phylogenetic perspective is helpful in enabling one to grasp how basic is interdependence as a principle of life. Figures 48–51 illustrate varieties of tiny plankton and bacteria

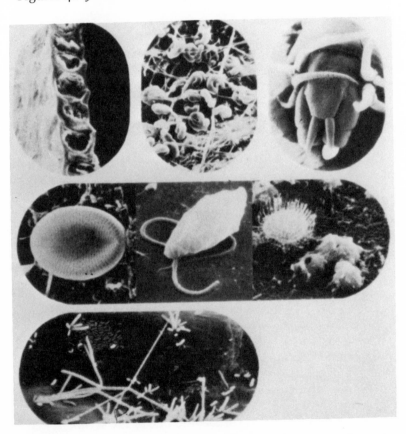

Figure 48. A variety of tiny marine organisms (from Sieburth 1975). Top, left to right: green alga, fungus, nereid worm; middle, left to right: diatom, flagellate, ciliate testaceans (amoeba with a house); bottom: bacteria

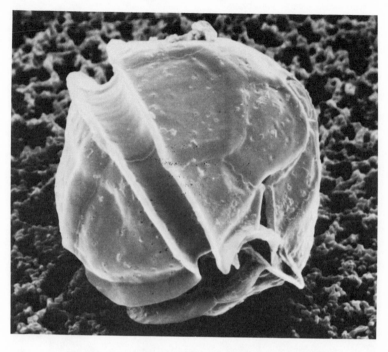

Figure 49. A dinoflagellate (from Sieburth 1975)

that inhabit the top millimeter of the ocean close to the energy-giving rays of the sun (Sieburth 1975). These organisms—algae, fungi, diatoms, and bacteria, too small to be seen with the naked eye—have been in the world somewhere between 500 million and a billion years, hundreds of millions of years longer than anything resembling man or any mammal. As early biological forms, however, they illustrate fundamental principles of nature that have persisted and retain important meaning for us today. These groups of unconnected cells are very closely interrelated. In fact, no one of the several species represented could survive without the others, because the nutrition and metabolic requirements of one are supplied in the waste products of another. As they need to live close to one another as well as within range of the sun's rays, they illus-

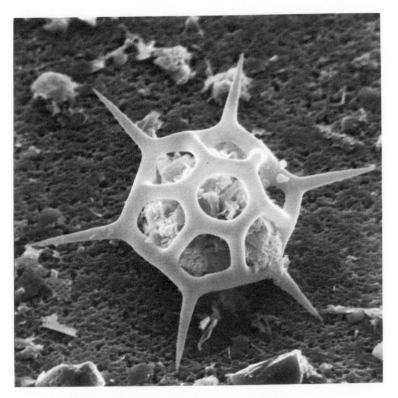

Figure 50. A silico flagellate (from Sieburth 1975)

trate the fundamental biological principle of interdependence. To the casual eye the behavior of these little creatures is ungoverned. They appear to be tossed about at random by the turbulence of the sea. The apparent lack of order is deceptive, however. They are kept together by a chemically-mediated biological attraction. We recognize their presence on the surface of the ocean as slicks.

The intercommunication and symbiotic behavior of separate unicellular organisms in proximity to one another are similar to those of specialized cells in the tissues of plants and animals higher on the phylogenetic scale; a metabolic event or tissue

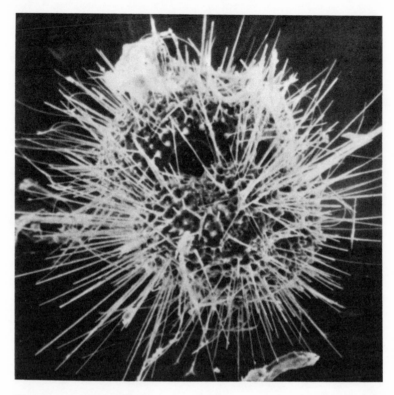

Figure 51. A foraminifer, an amoeboid protozoan in a calcarious house (from Sieburth 1975)

reaction occurring in one part of the organism may profoundly influence the behavior of cells in another part. Such interactions are especially evident in strategies for survival which in complex and highly organized mammals may involve several different organs and tissues. The response to an invading organism (a pathogen), for example, may include local and general alterations in vasomotor behavior, in temperature regulating mechanisms, in biosynthetic functions of lymphocytes and leukocytes, and in the absorptive behavior of the gut and the metabolic activities of the liver and kidneys.

Many of the particular biochemical adjustments that are necessary for the survival of the individual and of the species are common to organisms simple and complex all along the phylogenetic scale. Plants and animals engage in numerous metabolic and immunologic strategies that neutralize the destructive effects of pathogenic forces and thereby preserve life. The strategies are served by a variety of inducible enzymes and chemical transformations. For example, when the roots of plants are deprived of oxygen because of flooding, most will switch to an oxygen-free metabolism (anaerobic glycolysis) with the ultimate production of ethyl alcohol (Crawford 1978). The potentially damaging effects of the resulting concentrations of ethanol are well tolerated by plants for short periods. Such a metabolic strategy would not, however, be suitable for water-dwelling plants. Those plants that are well adapted to wetlands, such as water lilies, undertake instead a series of biosyntheses remarkably similar to those performed by the nutritionally deprived or otherwise compromised mammalian liver (Tholen and Bigler 1962). Thus, not only regulatory molecules but entire chemical adaptive processes are common to widely diverse living creatures.

REGULATORS OF CELLULAR FUNCTIONS

A phosphate-containing molecule, a nucleotide called cyclic AMP, when excreted by certain soil bacteria causes single-celled amoeba-like slime mold organisms to aggregate and assume, for a time, a multicellular state in which the creature moves about, with each of the newly coupled cells functioning as a component of the whole. Throughout the phylogenetic scale from unicellular organisms to man, cyclic AMP turns up as a regulator of cellular activity. The other various chemicals that govern behaviors both in the simple systems of invertebrates and in complex mammalian systems consist mainly of certain organic chemicals, predominantly steroids, nucleotides, and polypeptides. Among the latter, the prostaglandins, which in man regulate the contractile activity of small blood vessels and a variety of secretary functions, are found in living forms at every level of development extending as far back as the Gorgonian Coral polyps that originated at least 425 million years ago.

Even an identical molecular structure may trigger responses of different sorts in organisms widely divergent along the course of biological evolution. For instance, the neurotransmitters serotonin, gamma amino butyric acid, glycine, and others, as well as the hormones, such as prolactin, and the numerous steroids, are at work all along the course of biological evolution serving widely divergent functions in specialized organ systems. Indeed it is possible to conclude that throughout hundreds of millions of years of biological history relatively few new molecular structures have evolved. There have been some, of course, often consisting mainly of minor rearrangements in an amino acid sequence, but for the most part nature has utilized the same old molecules in different ways to accomplish widely differing and increasingly complex functions. Prolactin, for example, named for its importance in stimulating milk production in mammals, functions to regulate salt- and water-balance in sharks, animals whose biological design goes back at least 150 million years. In certain fishes, developed later, prolactin promotes the secretion of a mucous substance on the skin of the animal which serves as food for newly born fish, an intriguing precursor of lactation. As a further example, a steroid crustecdysone, which sets off moulting in insects, is excreted in the urine of female crabs (Kittridge et al. 1974). Dissolved in seawater it attracts male crabs, initiates their courting behavior, and achieves fertilization of the eggs. In humans, steroids, molecules closely related to crustecdysone, circulate in the blood as the male and female sex hormones to bring about growth and voice change in men and breast development in women.

Many behaviors are elicited by external chemical stimuli. In dogs, for example, not only mating but a whole repertoire of social behavior is subject to chemical regulation through smelling. The process requires that one or more molecules of a volatile odorous substance make contact with a specialized receptor on the surface of the nasal membrane of the animal. Olfactory nerve cells are activated, and they in turn commu-

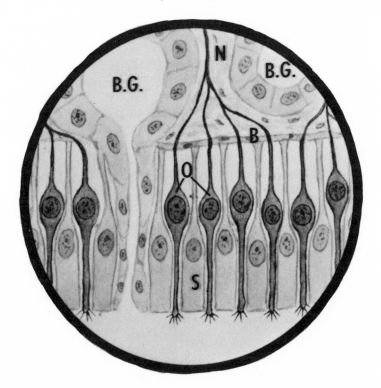

Figure 52. Specialized receptors on the nasal membrane (© 1953 CIBA Pharmaceutical Co., from *The CIBA Collection of Medical Illustrations*, by Frank H. Netter)

nicate through neurotransmitters, chemical mediators in the brain, to distant parts of the body where further cell-to-cell communications set in motion the several aspects of the animal's responsive behavior. Receptors throughout the body allow the attachment of the various regulator molecules to bring about one or another change in the cells' behavior.

Specialized receptors on the surface of cells are also involved in the action of drugs introduced into the body. Keyed only to specific receptor sites, they alter the behavior of certain tissues but have no effect on others that lack the suitable receptor sites.

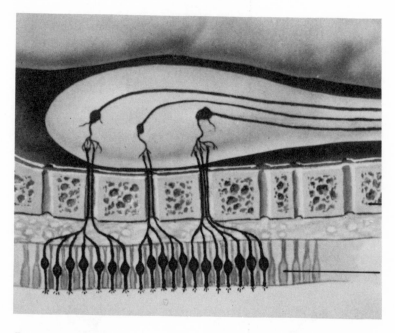

Figure 53. Synapses in the olfactory bulb that will carry smell sensations into the brain (© 1953 CIBA Pharmaceutical Co., from *The CIBA Collection of Medical Illustrations*, by Frank H. Netter)

Many of the regulatory chemicals found in animals are present also in the plant kingdom. Most of them serve either as attractants to insects to promote pollination, or as repellants to discourage potential predators. In either instance, the result is the regulation of social behavior to protect the individual organism, to achieve continuity of the species, and to effect harmonious interspecies balance.

DEVELOPMENT OF SOCIAL BEHAVIOR

In humans, the initiation of a chain of chemical communications leading to changes in the behavior of tissues, organs, and organ systems may respond to external chemical cues such as odors, but much more often it will be based on symbols, words, gestures, facial expressions, and other aspects of body language that require a complex process of interpretation. The process begins with the communication between mother and newborn infant, a creature who must be fed, protected, and cared for by another human being. The mother attends to these and other requirements necessary to ensure her infant's survival and proper growth. The infant develops the first corollary of interdependence, trust. In any social organization, mutual trust is basic to the predictability of outcomes of behaviors. It is the basis of mores, etiquette, and traditions.

The members of every social group bring to it their several individual genetic proclivities. As a group they are exposed to tangible forces in the environment, temperature, atmospheric influences, and toxins. Moreover, groups may have a characteristic nutritional behavior. They also evolve a set of community or group behaviors that express their interdependence and lead to equilibrium. Underlying their various activities are shared beliefs, values, and taboos from which evolve pressures to conform and sanctions or punishments for the nonconformist.

SOCIAL EXCLUSION

One of the most severe punishments for a nonconformist is exclusion from the group. A well-recognized consequence of complete social exclusion imposed under a variety of names by societies widely scattered over time and over the globe is sudden, unexplained death.

The ancient Greeks wrote a rejected citizen's name on a shell and threw it out to sea, thus ostracizing him. Certain tribal societies even today practice bone pointing or voodoo, or make "pouri pouri" with the same objective and the same consequence: death of the excluded one. In contemporary American society, individuals are not formally placed beyond the pale. Moreover, our sudden unexpected deaths are, by convention, designated as myocardial infarction (heart attack), despite the fact that at autopsy pathologists fail to find evidence of infarction in upwards of 50 percent of instances of sudden death (Schwartz et al. 1965; Baroldi, Falzi, and Mariani

1979). Such deaths are actually caused by disruption of the neural mechanisms that govern the heartbeat—a kind of suicidal imbalance of excitatory and inhibitory impulses. It may not be coincidental that deaths attributed to myocardial infarction are encountered with special frequency among those who have been recently bereaved (Parkes 1967; and Rees and Lutkins 1967), cut off from important interdependent relationships, or otherwise emotionally drained (Bruhn, McCrady, and du Pleissis 1968; Wolf 1967). Depression has been correlated with poor prognosis in actual myocardial infarction, and there is much to suggest that fatal cardiac arrhythmias may be viewed more as a means of death than as a cause of death (Wolf 1969).

The mechanisms that underlie these grave developments depend on connections from the central nervous system that regulate the heartbeat (Schwartz et al. 1978). Like the other regulatory mechanisms already discussed, they operate through chemical messengers, in this case the neurotransmitters norepinephrine and acetylcholine at the nerve terminals and circulating epinephrine from the adrenal glands. The central circuits connected to the nerves of the heart ramify widely through the spinal cord and brain and, as pointed out above, are readily responsive to emotionally significant circumstances.

The fact that the heartbeat may be "turned off" by nerve impulses in the absence of intrinsic disease in the heart has hampered the assessment of one of the most important diseases of western society, coronary atherosclerosis, and its consequences. Precise diagnosis is further confounded by the lack of predictable correlation among the principal manifestations of coronary atherosclerosis—angina pectoris, congestive heart failure, arrhythmias of various sorts, sudden death, and even the location and obstructive nature of atherosclerotic plaques. A person may suffer from angina pectoris for years without ever experiencing a myocardial infarction. Indeed, he may have only minimal atherosclerosis in his coronary vessels. His pain, according to recent evidence, may be attributable to constriction of certain branches of the coronary arterial tree suffi-

Figure 54. Sisyphus in a painting by Titian

cient to produce a local shortage of oxygen. Prolonged coronary spasm has been shown to be capable of producing potentially fatal arrhythmias and of actually causing myocardial infarction (Maseri et al. 1978; Hellstrom 1979). More often myocardial infarction is associated with mechanical obstruction of the coronary vessels, perhaps accompanied by constriction at the time of the acute event. It has been amply demonstrated, however, that the likelihood of myocardial infarction or sudden arrhythmic death is not dependent on the degree of involvement of the coronary vessels with atherosclerosis. At autopsy, following death from accident or other causes, the pathologist may find extensive coronary atherosclerosis without the patient having suffered any manifestations of coronary disease during life.

The clinical features of what is conventionally called coronary disease appear to depend not only on the presence of underlying atherosclerosis but also upon dynamic events in the central nervous system that reflect the patient's way of life, his temperament, emotional state, and style of dealing with day-to-day problems and challenges. Meyer Friedman and R.

Figure 55. Sisyphus as represented on an ancient Greek vase

Rosenman (1959) have identified as "Type A" a behavior pattern characteristic of those who are vulnerable to the ravages of coronary heart disease. In much less extensive studies carried out at the same time and independently of those of Friedman and Rosenman, my colleagues and I observed a very similar pattern which we designated as the "Sisyphus reaction" because, like Sisyphus, the typical coronary patient was striving against odds and irrespective of his success was not able to relax and enjoy the satisfaction of achievement (Wolf 1969). Two artistic interpretations of the labors of Sisyphus are shown in figures 54 and 55.

ADAPTIVE STRATEGIES

However complex may be the factors involved in the social equation, the emotions experienced and the ways in which the body responds are limited to certain alternatives or series of options. Those involving skeletal muscles or internal organs are in a sense prescribed by the prevailing circumstances. The laboratory observations on humans reviewed in Chapter 3 showed clearly that symbolic stimuli growing out of interpersonal relations can alter in a major way the behavior of organs and organ systems as well as that of the whole individual. The ability of people to achieve healthy relationships and to accommodate themselves to change depends on what has been called the plasticity of the nervous system, that is, the ability to alter functional connections among associated neurons and to select appropriately among alternate behavioral pathways.

SOCIAL INTERACTIONS AND PATTERNS OF BODILY CHANGE

Unlike the ants and the bees, humans do not have a rigidly preordained role in society, but must continually select among a vast array of options that offer abstract as well as concrete rewards and punishments. Since social attitudes, values, rewards, and taboos have differed and changed from time to time and from culture to culture, it follows that prevailing symptoms and diseases should differ from era to era over the course of history. As Henry Sigerist, the medical historian, has pointed out, there have indeed been differences in prevailing patterns of illness from era to era. In Western Europe, for example, plague and leprosy were dominant in the Middle Ages, giving way to syphilis in the Renaissance. In turn, scurvy and ergotism were prominent in the Baroque period, and in the Romantic era, tuberculosis. "In every epoch," writes Sigerist, "certain diseases are in the foreground and . . . are characteristic of this epoch and fit into its whole structure. It seems as though the powers that ordain the style for and stamp their impress upon a certain epoch affect even disease" (Sigerist 1932, p. 180).

Several colleagues and I had an opportunity some years ago to study the impact of a social environment on human subjects who were resident on a research ward where on a daily basis a wide range of chemical substances in the urine and feces were analyzed, while diet and exercise were kept uniform (Schottstaedt et al. 1958, 1959, 1963). The social interactions among the fifteen to twenty long-term inhabitants of the ward were carefully observed and recorded. Those responsible for recording behavior and emotional responses were kept ignorant of the laboratory findings.

The metabolic ward had the special characteristics of a well-defined community with its own pressures, values, prestige points, and taboos. In short, it had established its own social equilibrium. Even transient disruptions of the equilibrium were found to be associated with substantial measurable metabolic changes.

Major metabolic changes in terms of urinary excretion of water, sodium, potassium, calcium, nitrogen, and creatinine occurred repeatedly in situations of stress among the patients. Deviations in excretion of metabolites of greater than 2.0 S.D. occurred on 60 of a total of 213 patient-days for which data were available. We found that the metabolic deviations correlated with the prevailing atmosphere of the ward. Many more occurred when the ward community as a whole was disrupted. Furthermore, a higher percentage of the stressful events were accompanied by metabolic changes when the ward was upset

STRESSES OCCURRING ON A METABOLIC WARD

	Ward Atmosphere		
	Quiet	Dis-turbed	Total
Stressful days on which meta-bolic data were available....	25	42	67
Non-stressful days on which metabolic data were available	78	68	146
Total patient-days on which metabolic data were available	103	110	213
Stressful days with significant metabolic deviations........	12	36	48
Non-stressful days with signifi-cant metabolic deviations....	7	5	12
% of stressful days with signifi-cant metabolic deviations....	48	86	72
% of non-stressful days with significant metabolic deviations................	9	7	8

Table 1. Metabolic deviations associated with stressful experiences on a metabolic ward during relatively serene circumstances contrasted with periods when the atmosphere of the ward was upset

as compared to when its atmosphere was relatively serene. Eighty-six percent of stressful events were accompanied by significant alterations in the balance data when the atmosphere of the ward was disturbed, while during relatively calm periods for the group as a whole only 48 percent of episodes rated as stressful were accompanied by significant changes. "False positives," or metabolic deviations of significant degree, occurred on only 12 of 146 patient-days which had not been independently judged as stressful.

Interpersonal difficulties among those with strong ties were much the most common sources of stress associated with metabolic deviations, accounting for 28 of the 46 stressful situations associated with such deviations. Interpersonal stresses arising between individuals without strong ties were less often associated with significant repercussions in the metabolic data. For example, the two most important interdependent relationships for Mr. H were with Miss R and Mr. T. All Mr. H's significant metabolic deviations related to interpersonal stresses occurred in association with situations arising in these two relationships. He also had difficulties in his dealings with Mrs. D, although they did not share close personal ties. But those episodes of conflict were not associated with significant metabolic deviations.

For several days the whole population of the ward reacted in a similar fashion. The nurses had been asked to submit to a psychological testing procedure and to evaluate the performance of one another in relating to individual patients. They proved to be reluctant and were personally threatened by the request. Throughout this period of uneasiness among the nurses, all of the patients under study on the ward displayed a uniform metabolic response consisting of a negative balance of all measured metabolites. The atmosphere of the ward was tense and subdued. There was no way to clearly characterize or quantify the psychological stimulus. In fact, the patients were unaware of the circumstances responsible for the nurses' anxiety.

Importance of Shape as well as Quantity

This experience illustrates that a bodily response to stress depends not so much on the quantity of the noxious stimuli but rather on the quality, or *configuration*, of the prevailing circumstances. Looking only for quantifiable data may cause one to miss the most pertinent evidence.

A vivid example of the importance of configuration in biology is evident in the contrast of smell and taste between spearmint and caraway. The terpenoid ketones (carvones) responsible for the distinctive aromatic character of each of these substances have identical composition and identical molecular weight and structure with one exception. The carvone molecule of spearmint is oriented to the right and that of caraway to the left. Thus, the two quite dissimilar spices are enantiomers (i.e., isomers) that are mirror images of one another (Russell and Hill 1971).

Many molecules have been assigned descriptive terms; the "double helix," for example, is used to describe the configuration of the nucleic acids, whose powerful influences may be greatly altered by a rearrangement of a single component amino acid. Their shapes and electrical charges are now explaining the action of chemicals in a way that a knowledge of their quantitative composition could never do. In medicine, we are just beginning to learn to move beyond our preoccupation with quantification and to ask configurational questions which enable us to explore a problem in more than one dimension. The configuration or pattern of an individual's adaptive response to a meaningful circumstance depends first of all on his perception, beyond that on the interpretive process in his brain, and finally on the character of the control mechanisms that express themselves as behavior.

Biological Equilibrium

The behavior of most systems is maintained in a steady state by recurrent or repetitive fluctuations and corrections. The patterning of recurrence may be more or less strictly timed or basically rhythmic. There are almost countless such rhythms in the living being from neural volleys whose period is in milliseconds to six-per-minute waves of arterial pressure variation, to three-per-minute fluctuations in gastric wall contractions, to the more obvious daily rhythms of eating and sleeping and walking, to biological fluctuations on a cycle of months and possibly years. The whole subject has been aptly dealt with in a publication of C. P. Richter on biological clocks (1965).

The principle of the constancy of the "milieu interieur" of Claude Bernard (1926) and the concept of homeostasis proposed by Walter Cannon (1932) express the careful balance of opposing forces like the excitatory and inhibitory interactions in the nervous system. I have already emphasized that wide fluctuations in certain bodily functions encountered under relatively stable circumstances seem to indicate vulnerability to disease.

Myriad body clocks set the level and the range of fluctuation of such functions as body temperature, blood pressure, hormone production, blood cell release from the bone marrow, and countless others. We speak of levels of all of these functions, but the levels are maintained by a rhythmic rise and fall that fluctuates widely at varying frequencies. Body temperature fluctuates on a twelve-hour cycle. The secretion of certain pituitary hormones and other body regulators fluctuate within a twenty-four-hour cycle. Some of the regulators operate by feedback control, others as oscillators. Wide fluctuations in the level of the regulated function would be expected in the former if there were a delay in feedback or an elevation of the threshold of a receptor. In the case of oscillators, Richter (1965) has suggested that normally those that control a certain function operate out of phase, thereby keeping the level of the variable fairly steady. He has hypothesized that undue fluctuations occur when, for some reason, the oscillators begin to synchronize. To illustrate, he refers to the work of R. G. Williams over forty years ago in which it was shown that in the normal thyroid gland the hormone-producing follicles are found in various stages of activity ranging from inactivity to full activity (Williams 1937–38). Under pathological conditions, on the other hand, all may be in a state of hyperactivity or all in total inactivity, resulting in either hyper- or hypothyroidism respectively. Such synchronous behavior of the follicles may be brought about by certain drug effects, infections, or perhaps by threatening life situations.

In a review of circadian rhythms, B. Rusak and I. Zucker (1979) have provided evidence that oscillators may be entrained by, or their periods or the amplitude of their fluctuation may be altered by, connections in the central nervous system. Thus, the oscillators may become participants in a person's overall adaptive behavior.

SOCIAL EQUILIBRIUM AND RAPID CHANGE

An effective social equilibrium, like bodily homeostasis, requires a neat balance of expressive behavior and restraint. Perturbations in the form of social change challenge the established interrelationships and adaptive capability of people in a society. To some extent, the continued stability of a tree in a windstorm will depend on the depth of its roots. Social systems are rooted in the past, in traditions, in shared values and goals. Rejection of the past and contempt for traditional values is hazardous to the health of the community and of the individuals themselves. When social change is so great as to amount to upheaval, the society is to an extent uprooted so that relationships become chaotic until new shared values and goals allow the establishment of a new equilibrium.

Nearly twenty-five centuries ago Hippocrates reminded his contemporaries of the risk of such drastic changes when he said, "Those things which one has been accustomed to for a long time, although worse than things one is not accustomed to, usually give less disturbance" (1938). While rapid change may be potentially noxious, nevertheless change is as essential for the growth of an individual as it is in the growth of social systems. The history of the world has been characterized by a continuous round of change and adaptation. At each point along the way, the quality of man's performance has reflected the validity of his values, his aims, his goals. In terms of social as well as bodily health, he has often been more unadapted than adapted, more sick than well.

Robert Williams, in his important book *To Live and to Die: When, Why and How* (1973), has explored with some of his colleagues the meanings and purposes of life and the significance of death and dying. Throughout, the focus is on social challenges and the hazards of changing values.

CHARACTERISTICS OF A HEALTHY SOCIETY

Apart from acknowledging the potentially pathogenic nature of radical change, it is important to ask what in any social structure are the specific elements that tend to promote health and longevity. The process of healthy adaptation for man involves his elaborate use of language and other symbols and reflects his special sensitivity about his place in the eyes of other men. As a tribal creature with a long period of development, he depends for his very existence on the aid, support, and encouragement of other humans. He lives his life so much in contact with others, and he is so deeply concerned about their expectations of him, that perhaps his greatest need is for their approval and acceptance.

Without question, a strong sense of group identity, a feeling of being needed and valued, is an important requirement of individuals in a healthy society. As already pointed out, in the early 1960s the town of Roseto in eastern Pennsylvania was found to be remarkably healthy and comparatively free of the major scourges of America, cardiovascular and mental illness (Bruhn and Wolf 1979). The striking feature of Roseto was its social structure. Because the Italians were initially shunned by the mainly Anglo-Saxon inhabitants of the region, their natural cohesiveness was actually accentuated. Not only were the family units extremely close and mutually supportive, but so was the community as a whole, so that there was essentially no poverty and virtually no crime. The male-female relationships in Roseto were those of the "old country" with the man the undisputed head of the household. Moreover, the elderly were respected and listened to. Both men and women lived to old age, and indeed the death rate among women was slightly greater than that among men, leading to the unusual presence in the community of a few more widowers than widows.

Sula Benet, a professor of anthropology at Hunter College, tells of the remarkable health and longevity of the Abkhasians of Georgia in the U.S.S.R. (1965). She emphasizes pecularities of that culture similar to Roseto: "the high degree of integration in their lives, the sense of group identity that gives each individual an unshaken feeling of personal security and continuity and permits the Abkhasians as a people to adapt themselves—yet preserve themselves—to the changing conditions imposed by the larger society in which they live" (p. 104). The resemblance of the prevailing philosophy of Roseto is evident.

Also in common with Roseto, and in contrast to most American communities, the place of the elderly in the community of Abkhasians is very special. Benet writes that as "a life-loving, optimistic people, [they are] unlike so many very old 'dependent' people in the U.S. who feel they are a burden to themselves and their families—they enjoy the prospect of continued life. . . . in a culture which so highly values continuity in its traditions, the old are indispensable in their transmission. The elders preside at important ceremonial occasions, they mediate disputes and their knowledge of farming is sought. They feel needed because . . . they are" (p. 27). The similarity to the situation of the elderly in Roseto is striking.

The challenge for modern society, then, is to preserve insofar as possible the salubrious influence of established values of mutual concern in the face of inevitable and increasingly rapid change. Another important requirement of individuals in a healthy society is their constructive interdependence. Among the microscopic forms in the top millimeter of the sea, interdependent aggregations of single-celled animals must surely be the forerunners of tissues. In tissues, cells are not only bound together in a fabric but they perform specialized functions that contribute to the viability and welfare of the whole structure. Perhaps one sees best in cities the tissue of human society. The mass of humanity on the face of the earth may be comparable to the organisms in the top millimeter of the sea. We recognize then the interrelatedness of all life and hence the identity of life above and apart from individual identity.

THREATS TO HEALTHY ADAPTATION

It is further evident that human beings are threatened by those very forces in society upon which they are dependent for nourishment, life, and happiness. They must be part of the tribe, and yet they are driven to give expression to their individual proclivities; because of their sensitive organization they are often pulled two ways at the same time. Events having to do with an individual's place in society take on major significance for him, and he often functions best when his own ends are totally subordinate to the common end, the "team approach" in modern parlance. Conversely, when frustrated in such efforts, or rejected by his group, the individual may get sick or even die. Not only is he jeopardized by those forces that threaten survival of self and kin and opportunities for procreation, but also he is endangered when, through the actions of others, his growth, development, and expression of individual proclivities are blocked, and often when his aesthetic needs and creative potential are not fulfilled. Further, man's lively appetite for challenge, exploration, and adventure, by driving him into situations fraught with difficulty and hardship, may yield frustration and enhance vulnerability. Threats to his ability to perform in all of these spheres constitute the important everyday stresses that contribute to many varieties of disability and disease.

We conclude then that as man needs to live in a fashion acceptable to his fellows, he needs to derive spiritual nourishment from his associations as well as from his activities and achievements. He needs to satisfy in some way his various emotional yearnings, including his unquenchable thirst for power and prestige, and to realize his potential for love and for creativity.

The ability to hope and to trust in those about one, the ability to have faith in one's destiny and to realize one's personal identity—these are the elements of emotional security that can sustain an individual and a society through all manner of hazards and hardships.

Coda

This book has attempted to present a unified concept of behavior, pointing out, first of all, that the functions of the various internal organs of the body are integrated with those of the skeletal muscles and both are subject to regulation by the same mechanisms in the nervous system and elsewhere in the body. That is to say that the autonomic and somatic nervous systems are not separate at all but act as parts of a unified mechanism that expresses as behavior, responses to external events and to inherent drives, attitudes, values, and preferences. In highly-developed living creatures, these vital mechanisms are maintained by central controls in a state of dynamic equilibrium capable of responding to challenges, concrete and symbolic. Health, therefore, reflects the quality of the adjustments, and disease implies a failure of effective adaptation, usually in the form of responses that are inadequate, excessive, or otherwise inappropriate. Furthermore, it is the inappropriate response of cells, tissues, or general behavior that constitutes the very manifestations of disease.

Experimental evidence for these propositions has been reviewed and emphasis has been placed on interdependence at every level of biologic organization, including social relationships. At each point on the scale from free living cells to highly complex multicellular organisms, the nature of interrelationships determines well-being and survival on the one hand, and disease, disability, and death on the other.

References

Andersen, H. T. 1963. The reflex nature of the physiological adjustments to diving and their afferent pathway. *Acta. physiol. scand.* 58:263.

Baroldi, G; G. Falzi; and F. Mariani. 1979. Sudden coronary death: a postmortem study in 208 selected cases compared to 97 "control" subjects. *Amer. Heart J.* 98:20–31.

Benet, S. 1965. *Abkhasians: the long living people of the Caucasus.* New York: Holt, Rinehart, and Winston.

Bergman, S. A.; J. K. Campbell; and K. Wildenthal. 1972. Diving reflex in man: its relation to isometric and dynamic exercise. *J. Appl. Physiol.* 33:27–31.

Bernard, C. 1926. *An introduction to the study of experimental medicine.* New York: Macmillan.

Bert, P. 1879. *Leçons sur la physiologie comparée de la respiration.* Paris: Baillère.

Blank, H., and M. W. Brody. 1950. Recurrent herpes simplex: a psychiatric and laboratory study. *J. Psychosom. Med.* 12:254.

Brown, W. L. 1938. Introduction to *Civilization and disease,* by C. P. Donnison. Baltimore: William Wood & Co.

Bruhn, J. G.; K. E. McCrady; and A. L. du Pleissis. 1968. Evidence of "emotional drain" preceding death from myocardial infarction. *Psychiatric Dig.* 29:34–40.

Bruhn, J. G., et al. 1974. Psychological prediction of sudden death in myocardial infarction. *J. Psychosom. Med.* 18:187–91.

Bruhn, J. G., and S. Wolf. 1979. *The Roseto story: an anatomy of health.* Norman, Okla.: University of Oklahoma Press.

Bruner, D. 1968. Personal communication.

Cannon, W. B. 1932. *The wisdom of the body.* New York: W. W. Norton & Co.

Chapman, L. F.; H. Goodell; and H. G. Wolff. 1959. Augmentation of the inflammatory reaction by activity of the central nervous system. *Arch. Neurol.* 1:557–82.

Crawford, R. M. M. 1978. Biochemical and ecological similarities in marsh plants and diving animals. *Naturwissenschaften.* 65:194–201.

Danilewski, B. 1875. Experimentelle beitrage zur physiologie des Gehirns. *Pflugers Arch.* 11:128.

Donnison, C. P. 1938. *Civilization and disease.* Baltimore: William Wood & Co.

Dubos, R. 1951. Biological and social aspects of tuberculosis. *Bull. N.Y. Acad. Med.* 27:351.

———. 1953. The germ theory revisited. Lecture delivered at Cornell University Medical College, New York, 18 March.

Duncan, C. H., and H. C. Taylor, Jr. 1952. A psychosomatic study of pelvic congestion. *Amer. J. Obstet. Gynec.* 64:1.

Eliot, R. S.; F. C. Clayton; G. M. Pieper; and G. L. Todd. 1976. Influence of environmental stress on pathogenesis of sudden cardiac death. *Fed. Proc.* 36:1719–24.

Elsner, R., and B. A. Gooden. 1970. Reduction of reactive hyperemia in the human forearm by face immersion. *J. Appl. Physiol.* 29:627–30.

Engel, G. L. 1978. Psychologic stress, vasodepressor (vasovagal) syncope and sudden death. *Ann. Int. Med.* 89:403–12.

Fabrega, H. 1979. The scientific usefulness of the idea of illness. *Perspectives in Biology & Med.* 22:545.

Feigel, L. 1887. Sudden death from violent mental emotion. *Wiadomosci learskie (LWOW)* 1:297–301.

Feinstein, R., et al. 1977. Bradycardial response in aplysia exposed to air. *J. Comp. Physiol.* 122:311–24.

Friedman, M., and R. Rosenman. 1959. Association of specific overt behavior pattern with blood and cardiovascular findings. *J.A.M.A.* 169:1286.

Gebber, G. L., and Klevans, L. R. 1972. Central nervous system modification of cardiovascular reflexes. *Fed. Proc.* 31:1245–52.

Graham, D. T., and S. Wolf. 1950. The pathogenesis of urticaria: experimental study of life situations, emotions, and cutaneous vascular reactions. *J.A.M.A.* 143:1396.

———. 1953. The relation of eczema to attitude and to vascular reactions of the human skin. *J. Lab. Clin. Med.* 42:238.

Gunn, C. G.; M. Friedman; and S. O. Byers. 1960. Effect of chronic hypothalamic stimulation upon cholesterol-induced atherosclerosis in the rabbit. *J. Clin. Invest.* 39:1963–72.

Haldane, J. B. S., and J. G. Priestley. 1935. *Respiration.* London: Oxford University Press.

Hall, R. E.; Livingston, R. B.; and Bloor, C. M. 1977. Orbital cortical influences on cardiovascular dynamics and myocardial structure in conscious monkeys. *J. Neurosurg.* 46:638–47.

Halliday, J. L. 1948. *Psychosocial medicine: a study of the sick society.* New York: W. W. Norton & Co.

Hampton, J. W. 1965. Neuroregulatory mechanisms of blood clotting. *Bull. L. E. Philips Psychobiology Div., Mt. Sinai Hosp. Research Center* 13:21.

Harvey, W. P., and S. A. Levine. 1952. Paroxysmal ventricular tachycardia due to emotion: possible mechanism of death from fright. *J.A.M.A.* 150:479–80.

Heilig, R., and H. Hoff. 1928. Ueber Psychogenen entstehung des herpes labialis. *Med. klin.* 24:1472.

Hellstrom, H. R. 1979. Evidence in favor of vasospastic cause of coronary artery thrombosis. *Amer. Heart J.* 97:449–52.

Henry, J. P., and P. M. Stephens. 1977. *Stress, health and the social environment: a sociobiologic approach to medicine.* New York: Springer-Verlag.

Hernandez-Peon, R.; H. Sherrer; and M. Jouvet. 1956. Modifications of electrical activity in cochlear nucleus during "attention" in unanesthetized cats. *Science* 123:331.

Hetzel, B. S. 1964. Thyroid secretion in health and disease. *Aust. Ann. Med.* 13:80.

Hinkle, L E., Jr.; G. B. Conger; and S. Wolf. 1950. Studies on diabetes mellitus: the relation of stressful life situations to the concentration of ketone bodies in the blood of diabetic and non-diabetic humans. *J. Clin. Invest.* 29:754.

Hinkle, L. E., Jr., and S. Wolf. 1950. Studies of diabetes mellitus: changes in glucose, ketones and water metabolism during stress. *Proc. Assoc. Res. Nerv. & Ment. Dis.* 29:338.

————. 1952. A summary of experimental evidence relating life stress to diabetes mellitus. *J. Mt. Sinai Hosp.* 19:537–69.

Hippocrates. 1938. *Works of Hippocrates: medical classics.* Vol. 3. Baltimore: Williams & Wilkins.

Holmes, T. H., and R. H. Rahe. 1967. The social readjustment rating scale. *J. Psychosom. Res.* 11:213–18.

Holmes, T. H., et al. 1950. Springfield, Ill.: Charles C. Thomas.

Kakulas, B. A., and R. D. Adams. 1966. Principles of myopathology as illustrated in the nutritional myopathy of the captive Rottnest Quokka. *Proc. N.Y. Acad. Sci.* 138:90.

Katz, L. N.; S. S. Winston; and R. S. Megibow. 1947 Psychosomatic aspects of cardiac arrythmias: a physiological dynamic approach. *Ann. Int. Med.* 27:261–74.

Kittridge, J. S., et al. 1974. Chemical signals in the sea: marine alleochemics and evolution. *Fisheries Bull.* 72:1–11.

Koprowski, H. 1952. Latent or dormant viral infections. *Ann. N.Y. Acad. Sci.* 54:963–76.

Lazarus, R. 1976. *Patterns of adjustment.* New York: McGraw-Hill.

Levine, J. D.; N. C. Gordon; and H. I. Fields. 1978. The mechanism of placebo analgesia. *Lancet,* 23 Sept., pp. 654–57.

Lown, B.; R. Verrier; and R. Corbalan. 1973. Psychologic stress and threshold for repetitive ventricular response. *Science* 182:834–36.

Lynch, J. J. 1977. *The broken heart.* New York: Basic Books.

McKusick, V. A., and R. Claiborne, eds. 1973. *Medical Genetics.* New York: H. P. Publishing Co.

Maseri, A., et al. 1978. Coronary vasospasm as a possible cause of myocardial infarction. *New Eng. J. Med.* 299:1271–92.

Mittleman, B., and H. G. Wolff. 1939. Affective states and skin temperature: experimental study of subjects with "cold hands" and Raynaud's syndrome. *J. Psychosom. Med.* 1:271–92.

Parkes, C. M. 1967. Bereavement. *Brit. Med. J.* 3:232.

Pavlov, I. P. 1927 . *Conditioned reflexes: an investigation of the physiological activity of the cerebral cortex.* New York: Oxford University Press.

———. 1928. Lectures on conditional reflexes. Trans. by W. H. Gantt. New York: International Publishers.

Rees, W. D., and S. G. Lutkins. 1967. Mortality of bereavement. *Brit. Med. J.* 4:13.

Report of special task force to secretary of HEW. 1973. U.S. Government Printing Office.

Richet, C. 1881. De la contracture des hystereo-epileptiques. *Cong. Period. internat. d. sc. med. compt.-rend.* Amst. 6, pt. 2.

———. 1894. La résistance des canards a l'asphyxie. *C. R. Soc. Biol.* 1:244–45.

Richter, C. P. 1965. *Biological clocks in medicine and psychiatry.* Springfield, Ill.: Charles C. Thomas.

Rose, R. M.; C. D. Jenkins; and M. W. Hurst. 1978. *Air traffic controller health change study.* A report to the Federal Aviation Administration, Contract No. DOT-FA73WA-3211.

Rossier, J., et al. 1980. Distribution of opioid peptides in the pituitary: a new hypothalamic-pars nervosa enkephalinergic pathway. *Federation Proc.* 39:2555–60.

Rusak, B., and I. Zucker. 1979. Neural regulation of circadian rhythms. *Physiol Rev.* 59:449–526.

Rushmer, R. F., and O. A. Smith. 1959. Cardiac control. *Phsyiol. Rev.* 39:41.

Russell, G. F., and J. I. Hill. 1971. Odor differences between enantiomeric isomers. *Science* 172:1043–44.

Samter, M., ed. 1978. *Immunological diseases.* 3rd ed. Vol. 2. Boston: Little, Brown & Co.

Schmitt, G; H. Knoche; G. Junge-Hulsing; R. Koch; and W. H. Hanss. Über die reduplikation von aortenwandzellen bei arterielles hypertonie. 1970. *Z. Krieslaufforschg.* 6:481.

Schneck, J. M. 1947. The psychological components in a case of herpes simplex. *J. Psychosom. Med.* 9:62.

Schneider, R. A. ; J. P. Costiloe; and S. Wolf. 1971. Arterial pressures recorded in hospital and during ordinary daily activities: contrasting data in subjects with and without ischemic heart disease. *J. Chron. Dis.* 23:647–57.

Scholander, P. F. 1962. Physiological adaptation to diving in animals and man. Harvey Lectures. New York: Academic Press.

Schottstaedt, W. W., et al. 1958. Sociologic, psychologic and metabolic observations on patients in the community of a metabolic ward. *Am. J. Med.* 25:248.

———. 1959. Prestige and social interaction on a metabolic ward. *J. Psychosom. Med.* 21:131.

———. 1963. Social interaction of a metabolic ward: the relation of problems of status to chemical balance. *J. Psychosom. Res.* 7:83–95.

Schwartz, C. J., et al. 1965. Coronary disease severity and necropsy. *Brit. Heart J.* 27:731–39.

Schwartz, P. J., et al., eds. 1978. *Neural mechanisms in cardiac arrhythmias.* New York: Raven Press.

Seguin, C. A. 1956. Migration and psychosomatic disadaptation. *J. Psychosom. Med.* 18:404.

Sieburth, J. M. 1975. *Microbial seascapes*. Baltimore: University Park Press.

Sigerist, H. E. 1932. *Man and medicine*. Trans. by Margaret Galt Boise. New York: W. W. Norton & Co.

Simmons, L. W., and H. G. Wolff. 1954. *Social science in medicine*. New York: Russell Sage Foundation.

Skinner, J. E.; J. T. Lie; and M. L. Entman. 1975. Modification of ventricular fibrillation latency following coronary artery occlusion in the conscious pig: the effects of psychological stress and beta-adrenergic blockade. *Circulation* 51:656–57.

Smith, O.; R. B. Stephenson; and D. C. Randall. 1974. Range of control of cardiovascular variables in hypothalamus. In *Recent studies of hypothalmic function*, edited by K. Lederis and K. E. Cooper. Basel: Krager.

Smith, O., et al. 1979. Renal and hindlimb vascular control during acute emotion in the baboon. *Am. J. Physiol.* 236:198–205.

Stevenson, I.; C. H. Duncan; S. Wolf; H. S. Ripley; and H. G. Wolff. 1949. Life situations, emotions and extasystoles. *J. Psychosom. Med.* 11:257.

Straub, L. R.; H. S. Ripley; and S. Wolf. 1949a. Disturbances in bladder function in association with varying life situations and emotional stress. *J.A.M.A.* 141:1139.

———. 1949b. An experimental approach to psychosomatic bladder disorders. *New York J. Med.* 49:635.

Tholen, H., and F. Bigler, 1962. Pathogenetische beziehungen zvischen uramischem und hepatischem koma. *Deutsch. Med. Wochenschr.* 87:1188–92.

Treuting, T. F., and H. S. Ripley. 1948. Life situations, emotions and bronchial asthma. *J. Nerv. and Ment. Dis.* 108:380.

Twomey, J. J., and R. A. Good. 1978. *The immunology of lymphoreticular neoplasms*. New York: Plenum Press.

Uehlinger, E. 1970. Den krankheitswert der beginnenden S. Likose. *Int. Arch. Arbeitsmed.* 26:1–30.

Vaillant, G. E. 1979. Natural history of male psychological health: effects on mental health and physical health. *N.E. J. Med.* 301:1249–54.

Van Ree, M., and L. Terenius, eds. 1978. *Characteristics and functions of opioids.* Amsterdam: Elsevier.

Williams, R. G. 1937–38. Microscopic studies of living thyroid follicles implanted in transparent chambers installed in the rabbit's ear. *Am. J. Anat.* 62:1.

Williams, R. H., ed. 1973. *To live and to die: when, why and how.* New York: Springer-Verlag.

Wolf, S. 1947. Observations on the occurrence of nausea among combat soldiers. *Gastroenterology* 8:15.

————. 1949. Summary of evidence relating life situation and emotional response to peptic ulcer. *Ann. Int. Med.* 31:637.

————. 1959a. The pharmacology of placebos. *Pharmacol. Rev.* 11:689–704.

————. 1959b. *Placebos.* (Proc. Assoc. Res. in Nerv. and Mentl. Dis., vol. 37, pp. 147–61.) Baltimore: Williams and Wilkins Co.

————. 1965a. *The stomach.* New York: Oxford University Press.

————. 1965b. The bradycardia of the dive reflex—a possible mechanism of sudden death. *Trans. Am. Clinical and Climatological Assoc.* 76:192–200.

————. 1965c. Further studies on the circulatory and metabolic alterations of the oxygen-conserving (diving) reflex in man. *Trans. Assoc. of Am. Physicians* 78:242.

————. 1967. The end of the rope: the role of the brain in cardiac death. *Canadian Med. Assoc. J.* 17:1022–25.

————. 1969. Psychosocial forces in myocardial infarction and sudden death. Suppl. 4 to *Circulation* 39–40:74–83.

————. 1970. Evidence on inhibitory control of autonomic function. *Inter. J. of Psychobiology* 1:27–33.

————. 1978. Psychophysiological influences on the dive reflex in man. In *Neural mechanisms in cardiac arrhythmias,* edited by P. J. Schwartz et al. New York: Raven Press.

Wolf, S., and H. G. Wolff. 1942. *Human gastric function: an experimental study of a man and his stomach.* New York: Oxford University Press.

Wolf, S., and T. P. Almy. 1949. Experimental observations on cardiospasm in man. *Gastroenterology* 13:401.

Wolf, S., and H. G. Wolff. 1953. *Headaches: their nature and treatment.* Boston: Little, Brown & Co.

Wolf, S., and R. Pinsky. 1954. Effects of placebo administration and occurrence of toxic reactions. *J.A.M.A.* 155:339.

Wolf, S., et al. 1955. *Life stresses and essential hypertension: a study of circulatory adjustments in man.* Baltimore: Williams and Wilkins Co.

Wolf, S., and H. Goodell, eds. 1968. *Stress and disease.* 2nd ed. Springfield, Ill.: Charles C. Thomas.

Wolf, S., and B. B. Berle, eds. 1976. *The biology of the schizophrenic process.* New York: Plenum Press.

Wolf, S., and T. Wolf. 1978. A preliminary study in medical anthropology in Brunei, Borneo. *Pav. J. of Bio. Sci.* 13:42–54.

Wolff, H. G. 1953. *Stress and disease.* Springfield, Ill.: Charles C. Thomas.

————; T. H. Lorenz; and D. T. Graham. 1951. Stress, emotion and human sebum: their relevance to acne vulgaris. *Trans. Assoc. Amer.* Physicians 64:435.

Wundt, W. 1872. *Principles of physiological psychology.* Encyclopedia of Psychology, vol. 3. New York: Seaburg Press.

Index

A distinguished leader in American medicine and biology, Dr. Stewart Wolf currently is professor of medicine, Temple University, and vice president for medical affairs, St. Luke's Hospital, Bethlehem, Pennsylvania.

Dr. Wolf was born in Baltimore, Maryland, in 1914. After two years at Yale University, he transferred to Johns Hopkins and completed the premedical requirements within a year. In 1934, he was awarded a B.A. degree and in 1938, an M.D. His graduate training included experience in medicine and neurology at New York Hospital and Bellevue in New York City and at the Harvard Neurological Unit, Boston City Hospital.

After serving as a medical corps major in World War II, Dr. Wolf became associate professor of medicine at Cornell University Medical College in New York City. In 1952, he became the first full-time head of the Department of Medicine at the University of Oklahoma, a position he held for fifteen years. Simultaneously, he held professorships in physiology, neurology, psychiatry, and behavioral sciences. In 1967, he was appointed Regents Professor at the University of Oklahoma, a lifetime position.

After directing a research training program for seven years at Cornell, Dr. Wolf, upon moving to the University of Oklahoma, became head of the Neurosciences Section of the Oklahoma Research Foundation. In 1969, he organized and became director of the Marine Biomedical Institute of the University of Texas, Galveston, where important biochemical and neurobiological links between aquatic invertebrates and man were discovered. In 1977, he became director emeritus of the Institute.

Dr. Wolf founded the Tott's Gap Laboratories and Institute for Human Ecology in the foothills of Pennsylvania's Pocono Mountains in 1958. Today he is director of the Institute.

Dr. Wolf has served as a member and officer of many professional and academic societies and is the recipient of numerous awards, including those from the American Heart Association and the American Gastroenterological Association. An honorary M.D. degree was awarded to him in 1968 by the University of Goteborg, Sweden. He was also president of the Oklahoma City Symphony Society for five years.

Dr. Wolf is the author of many articles and books, some of which are cited in the References section of this volume. Throughout his distinguished career, he has built bridges between the basic sciences and medicine.